SKYE & LOCH
THE GUIDE BOOK

Published in 2009
by
Aird Trading, Aird House, Aird of Sleat,
Isle of Skye. IV45 8RN.
Author: Lynne Woods
Assistant Editor: Doug Vickers
Field Assistant: Anne Lamb

ISBN 978-0-9562126-0-3

Printed by Mayoh Press Ltd.

Cover picture: The Cuillin from Elgol by Grumpy George
www.grumpygeorge.co.uk

Introduction

Welcome to Skye and Lochalsh. "See it...Do it....Don't miss it" as it says on the front cover, is what this book is about. Its aim is to help you, the visitor, to make the most of this beautiful area. It would be impossible to list everything of interest or name every individual shop, hotel, gallery, craft outlet etc. However, what is hoped is that by taking you around the area, including "off the beaten track," you will have the pleasure of discovering for yourself many of the additional delights which were impossible to include here.

The book is divided into sections, arranged in a logical order for touring either part or all of Skye and Lochalsh. The map on page 6 identifies these sections. The numbers on this map correspond with the numbered sections of the book. Please note that the maps are not intended for precision navigation – their purpose is to illustrate the general location of those things mentioned in the text. Inside the back cover you will find a list of appropriate Ordnance Survey maps. There is also a list of useful telephone numbers. Public toilets are listed in red in most sections.

You will notice that in this part of the World many names have more than one spelling and that there is often more than one place with the same name. It all adds to the interest!
Whilst every attempt has been made to ensure accuracy, things do change with the creation of new enterprises and the disappearance of others as people retire or move on, a fact for which the publishers cannot accept responsibility.

It is hoped that you will enjoy using this guide and that you will take home with you many wonderful memories and a resolution to come again soon!

CONTENTS

Page no. (Red numbers refer to the Area Map on page 6.)

4. Skye & Lochalsh: An Introduction
6. Area map: Skye & Lochalsh
7. 1. South Skye - The Sleat Peninsula, Kylerhea and Kyleakin
14. 2. Central Skye - Broadford
17. 3. Central Skye - Strathaird & Elgol
22. 4. Minginish - The Cuillin and Glen Brittle
27. 5. Central Skye - Portree & Dunvegan
34. 6. Trotternish
42. 7. Waternish
46. 8. Duirinish
51. 9. Raasay
56. 10. Lochalsh
64. Useful information
Bibliography

SKYE & LOCHALSH: AN INTRODUCTION

The Skye and Lochalsh area is a unique and very special part of Scotland. Skye is the largest and most northerly of the Inner Hebrides. Fifty miles long, it is wild and remote, unspoiled, thrillingly rugged and breathtakingly beautiful. Lochalsh is so much more than simply the gateway to Skye: It is an area of awesome mountains and isolated glens where you are more likely to see deer than other humans. Much of the turbulent history of the Highlands was played out here. In Skye and Lochalsh history and legend have become so interwoven that past and present seem to constantly overlap. The remains of many former settlements chart the history of the various peoples who have lived here over the centuries.

Arriving by ferry ....

Skye: The Winged Isle....

Skye, so named by the Vikings, is also known as "Eilean a' Cheo" (The Isle of Mist) or "An t-Eilean" (The Winged Isle.) The latter hints at the island's almost magical qualities of air and light but also reflects its shape - long ribbons of land reaching out between dramatic sea lochs, each peninsula having its own distinctive character and nowhere being more than five or six miles from the sea. At the core of the island are the Cuillin Hills, some of the oldest rocks in the World, which rise majestically to over 3000' (900m) in a series of jagged ridges and peaks.

A turbulent history....

Evidence of settlement on Skye dates from prehistoric times. Mesolithic hunter-gatherers are known to have lived here but it was probably the Celts who first arrived in any great numbers. They travelled from Ireland to establish new communities and brought with them their own language, from which Gaelic is derived. This language still thrives on Skye and the Gaelic College, Sabhal Mòr Ostaig, is to be found here.

After the Celts, came the Vikings who were responsible for many of the Norse place names. Strong, guttural sounding names such as Fladday and Carbost have Nordic origins. Softer sounding words, such as Caluimcille, are Celtic.

Arriving by road....

The Vikings were eventually defeated by Alexander the Third in the middle of the Thirteenth Century. Only then did Skye become part of Scotland. The island came under the Earldom of Ross until it was divided between the four chiefs of Clans MacDonald, MacLeod, MacKinnon and Nicholson. The power struggle between the MacDonalds and the MacLeods led to many bloody battles and provided much of Skye's turbulent history. Successive governments tried to bring Scotland under central control. The Jacobites, including the majority of Highlanders, wanted to see the exiled Charles Edward Stuart (Bonnie Prince Charlie) crowned King of

SKYE & LOCHALSH: AN INTRODUCTION (CONT'D)

Scotland. At the Battle of Culloden in 1746 the Jacobites were defeated and the young Prince made his famous getaway through Lochalsh to Skye, the Outer Isles and then, with the help of Flora MacDonald, back to Skye before leaving for France never to return. The evocative "Skye Boat Song" tells the story. After Culloden, the clan system changed for ever. The Chiefs lost much of their power and became landlords rather than leaders. An emotive part of the area's history was the infamous "Clearances" when large numbers of people were evicted from their homes to enable the landowners to utilise the land more profitably for grazing sheep. Thousands of Highlanders were forced to emigrate before an uprising led to the establishment of the crofting laws which ensured that the crofters were allowed to own their own land.

The people....

The crofting system endures today. Many people run small holdings, sometimes as their main employment but more commonly to supplement income from other sources. Tourism is now one of the main industries, along with traditional fishing as well as fish farming. Skye has its own whisky distillery and a large number of people produce high quality art and craft work in small studios and workshops. The combined population of Skye and Lochalsh is currently around twelve and half thousand, much fewer than before the Clearances, but this is swelled considerably in the summer months by the influx of tourists.

The wildlife....

The sparsity of the population, even in the busy summer months, means that the area is essentially a peaceful place where there is room for everyone. Similarly, the vast range of wildlife attracted to the various island habitats can exist in peace, largely undisturbed by their human counterparts. The sea is the playground of minke whales, dolphins, porpoises and basking sharks. Overhead soar a wide variety of birds, including Golden Eagles and the rare Sea Eagle. Large colonies of sea birds breed amongst the cliffs and on some of the nearby smaller islands the elusive puffin can be found.

"......explore at ones own speed."

Something for everyone....

The area enjoys a rich cultural life. In addition to the many artists who reside here, there is a thriving folk music tradition and several festivals are held throughout the year. Despite the rural nature of the landscape and the simplicity of the villages and tiny hamlets, there are several top class hotels offering the highest standards of hospitality and excellent restaurants serving local produce and seafood.

For some, this is the place to enjoy outdoor activities such as walking, climbing, sailing or sea kayaking. Some are attracted by the wildlife, while those interested in antiquities find it one of the best places in Britain to unearth the past. For others, it is simply a place to find ones own space, to explore at ones own speed and to find the peace and tranquillity which is Skye and Lochalsh.

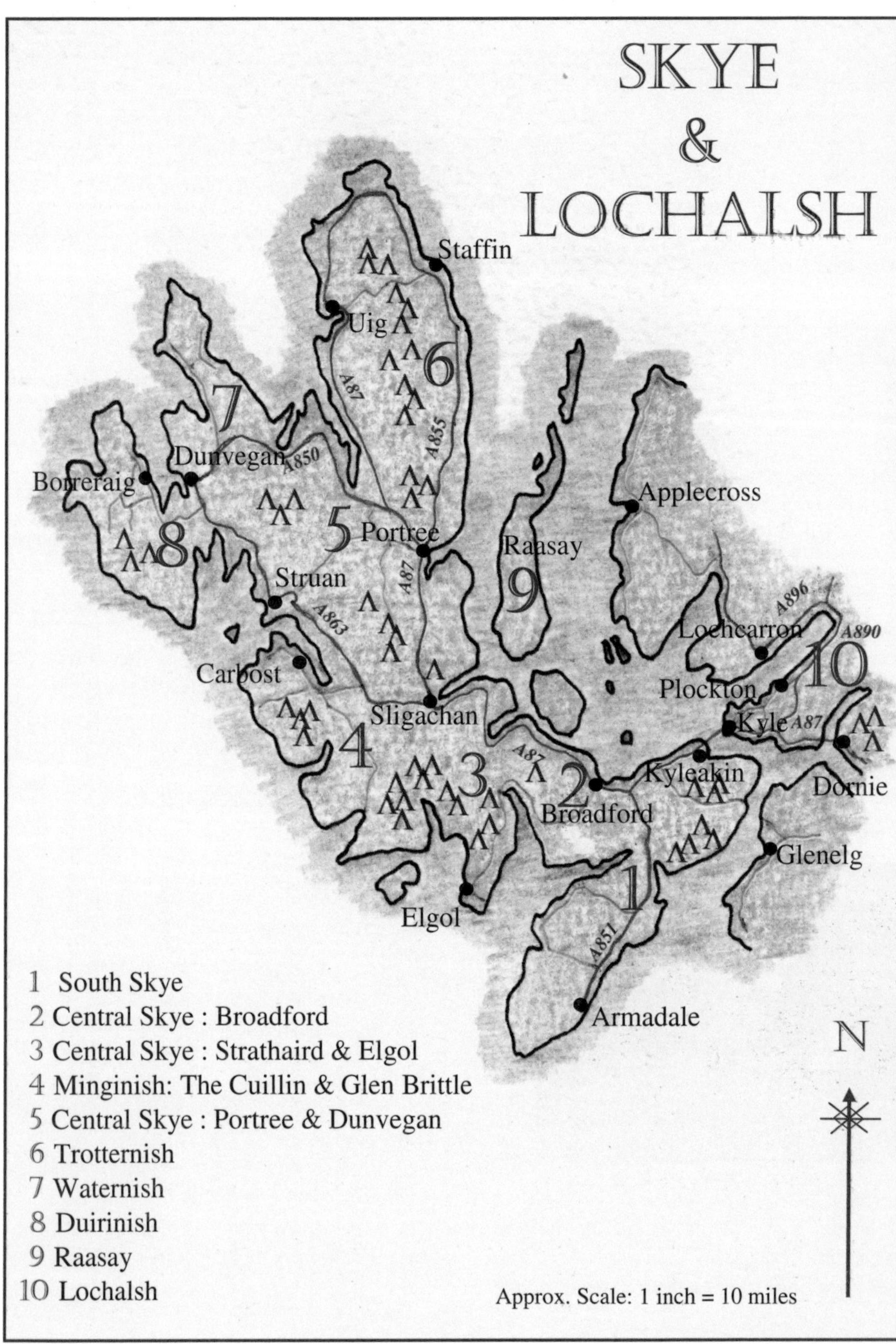
SKYE
&
LOCHALSH
Staffin
Uig
6
A87
A855
7
Dunvegan
A850
Borreraig
8
5
Portree
Raasay
9
Applecross
Struan
A87
A863
A896
Lochcarron
A890
10
Carbost
Plockton
Sligachan
Kyle
A87
4
3
A87
2
Kyleakin
Dornie
Broadford
Glenelg
1
Elgol
A851
Armadale
1 South Skye
2 Central Skye : Broadford
3 Central Skye : Strathaird & Elgol
4 Minginish: The Cuillin & Glen Brittle
5 Central Skye : Portree & Dunvegan
6 Trotternish
7 Waternish
8 Duirinish
9 Raasay
10 Lochalsh
N
Approx. Scale: 1 inch = 10 miles

1. SOUTH SKYE - THE SLEAT PENINSULA, KYLERHEA & KYLEAKIN

Whilst other parts of Skye are known for the grandeur of their wild landscapes and rugged peaks, South Skye is of a more gentle nature. The Sleat Peninsula must surely be one of Britain's best kept secrets. Its name (pronounced "Slate") is Norse for "level land." However, this is only in comparison with other areas. The milder climate here supports woodland and a wider variety of plant life, hence the nickname "The Garden of Skye." It is a magical place of sunsets and rainbows. Deer roam freely and buzzards, peregrines and sparrowhawks fly high above the moorland. Dolphins and porpoises swim up and down the Sound of Sleat.

To the west are unsurpassed views of the Cuillin Hills. To the south and west are the islands of Eigg and Rum. In the distance is the Ardnamurchan Peninsula. To the east, across the Sound of Sleat, are the white sands of Morar and tantalising glimpses into Loch Nevis and Loch Hourn which nestle either side of Knoydart, one of the remotest parts of mainland Britain.

This part of Skye has long been dominated by the Clan MacDonald. Sleat's ancient castles are the subject of many legends.

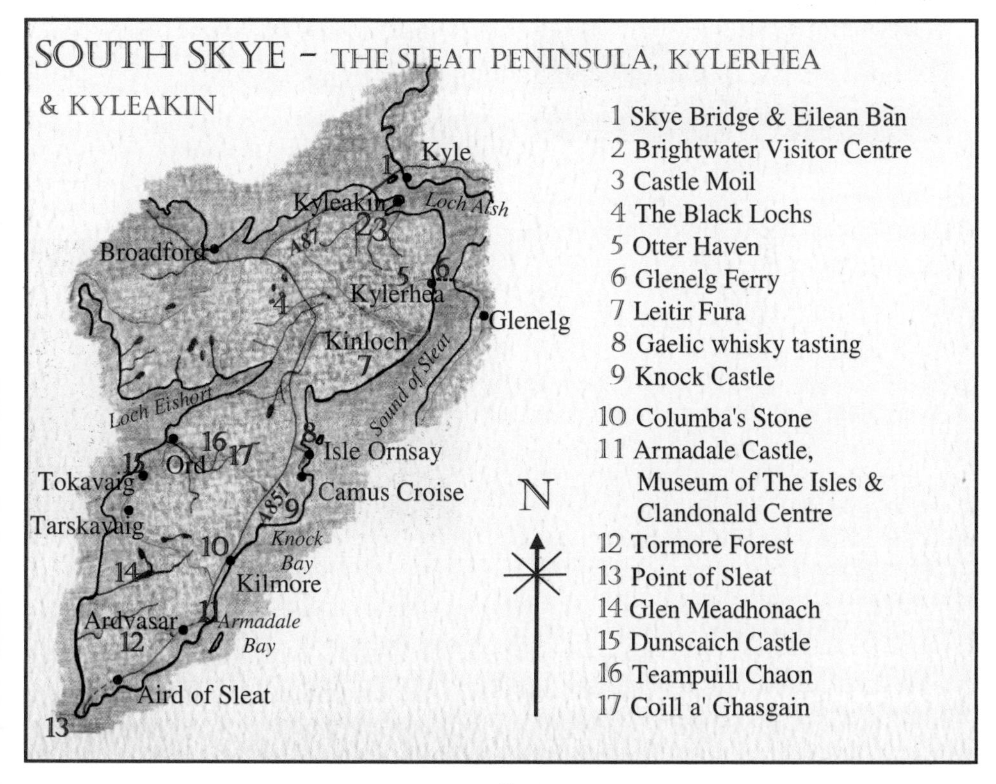

The area is not only a paradise for walkers, canoeists, sailors and wildlife enthusiasts but is also a thriving highland community. Crofting, the traditional practice of small scale agriculture, exists alongside modern living and the area can offer the very highest standards of hospitality and cuisine. There are galleries and studios, way-marked trails and an excellent museum.

In northern Sleat large tracts of moorland are traversed by the modern A851 but there are hidden gems to discover - tiny bays, a picturesque harbour, a miniature lighthouse, a deserted village and moody, black lochens.

Armadale.

For visitors who arrive by ferry across the Sound of Sleat from Mallaig, Armadale Bay is their first taste of Skye. At the pier

Armadale Bay

are gift shops, a superb pottery, an art gallery, a pleasant beach, "The Shed" - a tiny but excellent restaurant/takeaway and Skyelark, the shop/studio where the stunning photographs of "Grumpy George" are transformed into canvas prints.

Rubha Phôil is a twenty minute walk through woodland to a viewpoint from which seals can often be seen basking on the rocks below. Exhilarating wildlife spotting trips are available on the **SeaFari** boats. These often go into Loch Nevis or to the island of Eigg.

Armadale filling station, owned by the community, houses the local post office and offers tourist information as well as souvenirs, books, coffee and soft drinks.

Several woodland walks are detailed on the nearby information board. For those who have not arrived by ferry, a trip across to the busy fishing port of **Mallaig** is an interesting excursion.

Just over half a mile from the pier are the ruins of **Armadale Castle** and the **Clan Donald Centre**. Here an enjoyable afternoon can be spent strolling round beautiful gardens and woodland nature trails. In the castle grounds is the **Museum Of The Isles**. From a prehistoric stone circle inside the entrance, visitors are taken forward in time through five centuries of Norwegian rule to the present. A genealogy centre

The Museum of The Isles

provides information for modern-day MacDonalds wishing to trace their ancestry. At the entrance to the gardens is a licensed restaurant, gift shop and small garden centre.

Buses leave Armadale for other parts of the island but there can often be a long gap between buses! A good taxi service is available.

Ardvasar

Ardvasar is the largest village on Sleat. Public toilets can be found at the community centre. There is a well stocked food store/off licence and several B and Bs. The **Ardvasar Hotel** offers accommodation, food and the chance to take a leisurely drink whilst enjoying magnificent views. The boatyard of **Isle of Skye Yachts** occupies a picturesque setting and, in addition to yacht charter, offers repairs and other facilities for seafaring visitors.

Tormore Forest

A mile or so south of Ardvasar, Tormore Forest provides a sheltered track which leads up through the trees for a pleasant, dog-friendly walk.

Aird of Sleat

Beyond Ardvasar, the three miles to the Aird of Sleat bring ever more spectacular views around each bend. Keen-eyed visitors may spot by the side of the road **The Maiden's Stone** – a large boulder with a hollow in the top. A legendary witch laid a curse on the local cattle, affecting their ability to yield milk. To appease the witch some milk had to be left in the hollow each week!

For dogs or cats in need of accommodation, **Aird Kennels and Cattery** is excellent and is highly recommended by local residents Molly Black Labrador and Megan Cairn Terrier!

At the end of the road are **Aird Old Church Gallery** and a car park for those wishing to continue on foot the remaining two miles to **The Point of Sleat**, the southern tip of Skye where there are the remains of a tiny harbour. The original Sleat lighthouse was unfortunately replaced with a modern automated structure in 2003. From The Point are panoramic views sweeping from Mallaig, past the white sands of Morar and distant Ardnamurchan Point, to the islands of Eigg and Rum.

The Point of Sleat

Sabhal Mor Ostaig

Travelling north on the A851 from Ardvasar, the Gaelic college is situated at Kilbeg. Students can study the Gaelic language and gain qualifications in Business and Media Studies. Gaelic is still spoken extensively throughout the islands.

Tarskavaig

From the A851 at Kilbeg, a picturesque single track route meanders to the western side of the peninsula before eventually rejoining the main road further north. After just over a mile, near its highest point, a track to the left leads to **Glen Meadhonach**, a beautiful place where ancient native woodland survives and Skye's only "canal" at Dalavil connects **Loch a Ghilinnie** to the sea. The curious slow worm, more snake than worm, can sometimes be seen along the path and around the loch the air is often alive with dragonflies. The way leads close to the deserted village of **Caradal**, whose inhabitants were evicted towards the end of the Nineteenth Century.

On the way to Tarskavaig

The road to Tarskavaig continues down passed **Loch Dhughaill**, a small and particularly pretty loch. Brown trout is fished here. (Permits are available from the Clan Donald Centre.)

The settlement of **Tarskavaig** nestles behind a sandy beach and is one of several coastal settlements to which people were evicted during the Clearances. It is a typical crofting settlement. From **Tarskavaig Bay** there are stunning views across to Rum. For paintings with a difference, or unusual textile art, visit **The Blue Studio**. For delicious venison, salmon and cheese visit the **Garden of Skye Smokehouse**.

Tokavaig

A place to linger - explore the shoreline, savour views of the Cuillin and admire the ash, cherry, hawthorn and birch which thrive in an ancient druid grove. On the headland is Skye's oldest castle, **Dunscaich.** Originally a Norse fortress, many legends surround the "Fort of Gloom." Said to have been built in a single night, it is also reputed to have been the home of the warrior queen who taught Cuchullin (after whom the Cuillin Hills are named) how to succeed in battle. A huge boulder nearby is said to be the rock where Cuchullin's dog, Luath, was tethered. Dunscaich was a MacLeod stronghold until taken from them by the MacDonalds who continued to live there until the early Sixteenth Century. It is now in a dangerous state of disrepair. A nearby burial mound is thought to be the last resting place of clan chiefs. Early Twentieth Century excavations unearthed a circle of chambers, each containing a skeleton in a sitting position.

Dunscaich Castle

Ord

On the edge of **Loch Eishort** and with views across to the mountains, Ord is one of the best places for the dramatic sunsets which appear to set the Cuillin alight. The shoreline is popular with seals. The entrance to a delightful private garden, sometimes open to the public, is at the bottom of the hill. Further up, on the left, are the remains of **Teampuill Chaon** which was an Eighth Century chapel dedicated to St. Comgan. Three miles further on is **Coîlle a' Ghasgain**, a wood where sanctuary from pursuit could be claimed – regardless of the crime committed.

The minor road rejoins the A851 just north of Knock Bay.

Kilmore

A church has stood on this site since the Thirteenth Century. The present one dates from 1876. Nearby are the ruins of a church built in 1681 and an ancient burial ground where MacDonald Chiefs were laid to rest. On the shore below is **Columba's Stone**, marking the spot where St. Columba is said to have landed around 585AD and blessed the site.

Knock Bay

Half way up the Sound of Sleat is Knock Bay, a beautiful, half-moon shaped bay from which there are stunning views across to the mountains of Knoydart. On the edge of the bay are the ruins of **Knock Castle** ("Caisteal Camus.") which was built by the MacLeods in the Fourteenth Century but taken from them by the MacDonalds in one of the many skirmishes between the two clans. Now in ruins, much of the stone was used to build nearby Knock Farm. A "green lady" is said to haunt the ruins. (Park by the main road.)

Nearby is the **Toravaig House Hotel**, a country lodge hotel with log fires and magnificent cuisine. A stay at this, or the nearby sister hotel **The Duisdale House Hotel,** offers the chance to experience this beautiful area from a different angle – a day sail aboard the hotel's own yacht.

Isle Ornsay (Eilean Iarmain)

Once the centre of Skye's fishing industry, from where barrels of herrings were sent all over the World, Isle Ornsay was also the port from which many

Isle Ornsay

emigrants departed. Later, with a regular steamer service, it became a tourist destination. The island's first public toilet (flushed by the tide) was built here in 1820. This natural harbour has an enchantment which seems to captivate all who arrive here: A cluster of whitewashed cottages and a hotel, reputed to be the most romantic in the World, overlook the tidal island of Ornsay, with its tiny lighthouse which was built in 1857. Gavin Maxwell, author of "Ring of Bright Water," once lived in the cottages adjoining the lighthouse. Alongside the hotel is the headquarters of **Praban nà Linne**, which markets a number of Gaelic named whiskies. Produced without chill-filtering, these hold a distinctive place amongst the connoisseur whiskies of the World. Tastings are available to visitors.

This is not a place to rush: Take time to sample the whisky; visit **Floaidh** for exquisite Harris Tweed clothing; admire the work of one of the visiting artists at the gallery **An Talla Dearg**, housed in what was once a grain store; enjoy a leisurely meal in beautiful surroundings – or simply sit and savour a unique atmosphere.

Camus Croise

Camus Croise is a lovely bay which provides inspiration to several artists who live there. Follow signs to their studios. Camus Croise is also home to **Skyak Adventures** – sea kayaking around Skye under expert supervision.

Kinloch

Kinloch means "head of the loch." A former shooting lodge of the MacDonalds, **Kinloch Lodge** is now home to the present Lord and Lady MacDonald and is run as a country house hotel and restaurant. Lady MacDonald is well known as a writer of Scottish cookery books.

Leitir Fura

The remains of this old village, abandoned in 1782, can be reached by walking from a car park at the end of a woodland track signposted from the A851. At the car park reconstructions show how these buildings were erected. Leitir Fura is a popular dog-friendly area with views down the Sound of Sleat to Isle Ornsay and beyond.

The Black Lochs

Alongside the modern A851 in northern Sleat much of the old single track road remains - providing an ideal place to stroll or cycle beside the Black Lochs, so called because of the colour of the water over underlying peat deposits. Water-lilies and dragonflies lighten the gloomy waters. In this area were once the shielings where cattle were taken for summer grazing and young men and women had the chance for romance at **Drochaid Airidh na Saorach** ("The Bridge of The Shieling of Courtship.")

Kyle Rhea

Kylerhea means "narrow place" and is the stretch of water which separates Skye from the mainland at its closest point. From the A87 a winding pass meanders through **Glen Arroch** into the heart of the hills with spectacular views of the mainland. This was once one of the main drove routes between the islands and the cattle markets of southern Scotland. Near the end of the road is a car park for the **Otter Haven** - a hide from which seals (or occasionally otters!) can be observed in the water below. The road ends at a landing stage from where a small, community-owned ferry runs in the summer to Glenelg on the mainland. Here the cattle would once have swum across, tethered together behind a rowing boat, often many hundreds at a time. (For **Glenelg**, see Lochalsh section.)

Following the old drove road

Public toilets can be found at Ardvasar Village Hall, Armadale Castle gift shop, The Otter Haven at Kylerhea & the King Haakon restaurant Kyleakin.

Kyleakin

Kyleakin (Gaelic: "Caol Acain") takes its name from **King Haakon IV** of Norway who sailed past here in 1263 on his way to the Battle of Largs. His defeat brought to an end centuries of Norwegian rule. Before the **Skye Bridge** was opened in 1995, this was where the Skye Ferry had arrived since 1841. Almost in the shadow of the bridge, Kyleakin offers spectacular views of the structure itself and of picturesque **Eilean Bàn Lighthouse.**

The village sits on a headland bounded by **Loch Alsh** and secluded **Loch na Beiste**. The ruins of **Castle Moil** lie above the harbour, facing the Kyle of Lochalsh. The MacKinnon Clan held the castle until the Seventeenth Century when it was abandoned. Legend tells of a MacKinnon chief who married a Norwegian princess, known as **Saucy Mary**, who demanded a toll from all passing ships. To enforce this she had a chain slung across the narrow straits. (The "saucy" part of her name came from the way in which she acknowledged payment: apparently she would lift her clothes to reveal her ample bosom to passing sailors!) The castle ruins can be accessed by a short walk from the far side of the harbour.

There are several bars and gift shops, a post office and small food store, restaurant and rows of pretty white cottages (Look out for the garden which is home to a large number of gnomes!) Kyleakin is popular with backpackers as there are hostels as well as hotels.

The shoreline is full of interest. Sea urchins can sometimes be found washed up amongst the pebbles and shells. Overlooking the fishing boats in the busy harbour and marina is a statue of a bronze otter by sculpture Laurence Broderick.

Nestling beneath the Skye Bridge, is

Kyleakin

Eilean Bàn ("White Island.") The cottages here were built to accommodate the lighthouse keepers. Later, author Gavin Maxwell lived here until his death in 1969. Today the cottages house a museum about Maxwell's life. The island is a nature reserve with viewing platforms, hides and a sensory garden. (Wheelchair friendly!) Tours of the island and lighthouse can be booked at the **Brightwater Visitor Centre** in Kyleakin where there are interactive displays about the island and its wildlife.

A shuttle bus runs over the bridge between Kyleakin and Kyle of Lochalsh.

Mhadaidh Ruaidh ("hill of the fox") near the bridge has way-marked walking and cycling tracks to the hilltop with jumps and boardwalks to make an exciting trail. From the viewpoint at the top there are unsurpassed views of Kyle, the Skye Bridge and over the Inner Sound with its many rocks and small islands. Behind are the mountains of Skye.

Nearby **Old Kyle Farm** is a rare breed centre (by appointment only.)

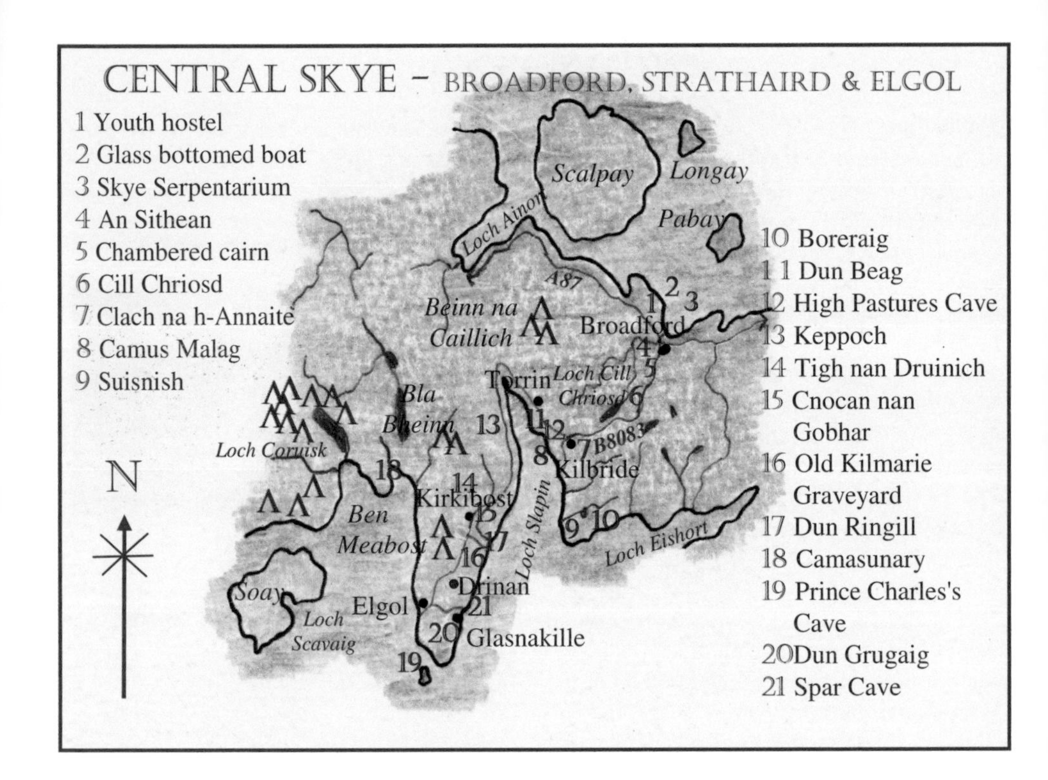

2. BROADFORD

Broadford, Skye's second largest settlement, forms the gateway between the island's gentle south and more rugged north. Sheltering beneath the charismatic Beinn na Caillich ("Hill of The Old Woman,") the village curves lazily around a sweeping bay, behind which the Applecross Peninsula forms an impressive backdrop to the islands of Pabay, Scalpay and Longay.

Broadford developed as a cattle market in the late Eighteenth Century but after the Kyleakin to Portree road had been built by Thomas Telford in 1812 it became the hub for routes to all other parts of the island. One fascinating, little-known fact is that it was from Broadford that the drink Drambuie had its origins: During Bonnie Prince Charlie's bid to escape Government forces in 1746, he was helped by Captain John MacKinnon of Broadford. In gratitude, the Prince disclosed the secret recipe for his own personal liqueur – "the yellow drink" which translates as "an dram buidhe." The MacKinnon family used the recipe for their own personal consumption for many years. During the late Nineteenth Century the drink was sold in The Broadford Inn and then in 1909 commercial production began in Edinburgh.

The majority of services can be found near the centre of Broadford. In addition to hotels, there are restaurants and bars, a twenty four hour filling station, a cash machine, bank, vet, a hospital and shops including a supermarket. Near the main car park are the Tourist

Information Centre and public toilets. Adjacent to the car park are pleasant sitting areas overlooking where the Broadford River flows into the bay. Otters may occasionally be seen playing in the water. In the winter months large numbers of red throated divers and other species arrive.
Over the bridge, past the **Broadford Hotel**, is a parade of shops including a small but well stocked general store, gift shops, a restaurant, a bank, a chemist and a post office. Beyond the post office is a computer centre where **internet access** is available. For a Sunday lunch feast The Broadford Hotel is an excellent choice!
A culinary experience not to be missed for those who are self catering is the locally caught seafood and shellfish which is available from **Isle of Skye Seafood Ltd.** on a small industrial estate to the north of the village, signposted from the main road.
Whilst most people visiting Skye stop at Broadford to make use of the facilities to be found here, there is also much of interest to justify a longer visit. There are several galleries, craft outlets and other tourist attractions. Older parts of the village, such as the old pier, are pleasant places to linger.

The Old Pier
Easily missed, the old pier is situated behind the Dunollie Hotel. Pleasure steamers en route for Portree once called here and the remains of old lime kilns bear testament to its past commercial use. Today it is a peaceful place with views to the islands in Broadford Bay. Situated at the pier are the **Sandbank Studio** of renowned local artist Duncan Currie, a second hand book shop and the studio of **"The Handspinner Having Fun"** which produces distinctive sweaters, rugs and yarns.

Fascinating galleries

The old pier, Broadford

The Far Pier
The village's second pier is accessed by a road close to the bridge over the river. It is an enjoyable walk along here with spectacular views across Broadford Bay towards Applecross and Wester Ross. Remains of a railway are those of the line which was once used to transport marble from the quarry at Torrin.
Glass bottom boat trips from this pier can be booked from the kiosk on the car park. The **Youth Hostel** can also be reached along this road.

Broadford Bay

Woodrising Photographic Gallery
An extraordinary collection of stunning photographs depicting in close up all aspects of Skye's unique landscape. Situated to the north of the village and signposted from the main road.

Skyeline Ceramics
A small working pottery producing beautifully quirky sheep and other figures in porcelain and stoneware. (Signposted from the main road.)

Skye Serpentarium
This is an award winning collection of snakes, lizards, frogs, iguanas and tortoises. Housed in sympathetic surroundings, the Serpentarium also acts as a refuge for reptiles which have been illegally imported or mistreated. (Since 1991 over 500 creatures have been rescued.) There is also an interesting gift shop as well as the excellent **Watermill Coffee Shop** serving home baking to eat in or take away. (Signposted from the main road, this is a good all-weather attraction and on fine days an excellent place to stock up on picnic goodies!)

Craft Encounters
Adjoining the post office is this gift shop which sells a wide range of high quality but reasonably priced gifts and souvenirs with a Scottish flavour.

Skye Jewellery
Stunning, exclusive jewellery which captures the essence of the Hebrides in beautiful Celtic designs. Each piece is hand crafted on the premises.

Creelers
A dining experience for true foodies! Creelers is a small but top quality restaurant and definitely one of the best places to sample the local shellfish, seafood and locally sourced meat and other produce. (Signposted from the main road.)

Three Herons Studio
Prints, photographs and paintings. (Situated next to the hospital and signposted from the main road.)

Local seafood

Public toilets can be found opposite the main car park in Broadford.

Strathaird & Elgol

To the north west of Broadford are Loch Ainort and the island of Scalpay. To the west the great Cuillin Hills beckon. However, to head there immediately would be to forgo the delights of Strathaird and Elgol and to miss one of the very best views of the Cuillin!
Strathaird is the promontory of land jutting out between Loch Slapin and Loch Scavaig. The road to Strathaird is hauntingly evocative. A peaceful and quiet place nowadays, it was once an area where several settlements flourished on soil made fertile by underlying limestone deposits. At almost every turn there is a footprint from the past. Layers of history are revealed in the form of chambered cairns, the ruins of several churches and hut circles marking sites where prehistoric dwellings once stood. From a later period are the ruins of buildings left abandoned during the Clearances of the Nineteenth Century.

An Sithean

A mile and a quarter along the B8083 Broadford to Elgol road is An Sithean, Gaelic for "**Fairy Knoll**" - a grassy mound to the west of the road. From this area came William Ross, one of the most famous Gaelic poets. Only twenty eight years old when he died in 1790, he had by then written much which later became traditional Gaelic poetry.

Chambered Cairn

About two and a half miles from Broadford the remains of a chambered cairn can be seen to the right of the road as it slopes down just before a left hand bend. Chambered cairns are stone burial chambers from Neolithic times. A central chamber often has smaller ones leading from it. Usually located near settlements, they were the equivalent of a modern graveyard. Sometimes the bodily remains would have been cremated.

Cill Chriosd

Overlooking a small loch by the roadside, Cill Chriosd ("Christ's Church") is what is left of a parish church originally built in the Sixteenth Century, to replace an even earlier structure. Cill Chriosd served the inhabitants of Strath until the "new" church was built in Broadford in 1840. Although it no longer has a roof, the walls remain largely intact. The MacKinnons and The MacInnes Clans once held authority in this area and many of them lie buried here.
An information board opposite the church details the geology, flora and fauna of the area.

Cill Chriosd

Loch Cill Chriosd

Loch Chriosd is a shallow loch which was dammed for fishing at the beginning of the Twentieth Century. It is a beautiful peaceful stretch of water, filled with reeds and other vegetation. Reed warblers and tiny dabchicks can be seen and during the winter months whooper swans from Iceland arrive here. The loch was reputedly home to a monster which would rise out of the water to take women and children from nearby until it was vanquished by a saint. The waters were subsequently deemed to have healing powers.

Kilbride

Kilbride ("St. Bridget's Church") is an interesting hamlet. Here can be found "**Clach na-h-Annaite"** ("Stone of the Chief Church.") A single eight feet high stone is thought to have once been part of a stone circle. Its name, however, has more recent origins: The farmhouse here was once the manse of MacKinnon clergymen who, father and son, held the office in a continuous line for one hundred and forty years.

Camus Malag

From Kilbride a tiny road signposted Loch Slapin meanders down to the small bay of Camus Malag. Cars can be parked on the grass here. To the north west are stunning views of Blaven (Blà Bheinn,) one of the Cuillin "outliers." To the south, the west coast of Sleat can be seen and on a clear day there are good views of the islands of Rum and Eigg. Where the road ends, a track continues two and half miles further to the headland Rubha Suisnish where the deserted village of Suisnish is a further reminder of the harsh treatment received from landlords during The Clearances. In 1853 thirty-two families were evicted from Suisnish. Watch out for Sea Eagles, which can sometimes be seen from this headland, before continuing along the track to **Boreraig,** the ruins of another "cleared" settlement.

Torrin

The name "Torrin" comes from the Gaelic for "mound" or "little hill." One could happily spend a day pottering around here, savouring the tranquil shores of Loch Slapin and the breathtaking view across to Blaven. The village is a crofting community where Gaelic is commonly spoken. Torrin is popular with summer visitors. There are various types of holiday accommodation, a small shop and cafe, an outdoor centre and a gallery. Whilst many parts of Skye have few trees and are consequently somewhat barren in appearance, on Torrin's fertile limestone soils trees and wild flowers, including several orchid species, flourish. Here also is found one of Skye's rare sandy beaches, close to which are the ruins of **Dun Beag**. There are many seabirds to be seen along the shore, including greenshanks and oystercatchers who gather here in large numbers. Seals, too, can often be seen.

At the quarry, Skye marble has been excavated since 1703 but there has been a community here for over two thousand years, evidence of which was discovered

The head of Loch Slapin

in 2006 at **High Pastures Cave.**

Blaven (Bla Bheinn) and Keppoch

After the B8083 rounds the head of Loch Slapin to the western shore there is a car park from which there is one of the best views of Blaven, Signposted walks from here go to Blaven ("the kindly mountain") or through woodland and then across open hillside to the deserted village of **Keppoch.** This was once home to forty-four families before they were evicted in 1852 and forced to emigrate to Australia.

The car park below Blaven

Hidden among the trees are the ruins of over twenty byres and cottages.

Tigh nan Druinich

Two miles along the road from the car park is a sign for "Tigh nan Druinich." In ancient times there was reputedly a house of this name ("house of fine craft") where fine jewellery and magical swords were produced. It is fitting, therefore, that the name "Tigh nan Druinich" has now been adopted by two modern day craftsmen who have chosen to establish workshops at Strathaird Steadings. So once again exquisitely worked swords are being lovingly forged here and high class jewellery crafted in Celtic designs.

Kirkibost

Meaning "the church near the farm," a track leads south east from here to **Cnocan nan Gobhair**, a large and well preserved chambered cairn. A road, signposted **Old Kilmarie Graveyard**, branches off for an interesting detour. Nearing the shores of Loch Slapin, adjacent to Kilmarie House, is a small iron gate leading to a tiny picturesque bridge over the river. Nearby is a grassy mound which is a superb example of a chambered cairn. The woodland path continues to the remains of **Dun Ringill**, once a stronghold of Clan Fingon (later the MacKinnons.) The entrance passage and the base of the walls can still be seen. Almost on the shore, behind a high wall, is the old graveyard. What was left of the church here was washed away by storms in the 1920's. However, it was also the site of a much older church – one of the chapels established by St. Maolrubha (also spelt Malrubha and several other

The path to Dun Ringill

ways too!) when he landed on Skye in AD673. A fine Celtic cross can be seen here.

From where the road peters out on the western shore of the loch a track continues to the townships of Drinnan and Glasnakille. The path affords views back into Loch Slapin, across to Loch Eishort and to the Sleat Peninsula. On returning to the B8083 the road climbs steeply along the lower reaches of **Ben Meabost** before revealing impressive views of the

Cuillin across Loch Scavaig.

Leaving Drinan

Elgol

Elgol lies at the southern tip of Strathaird, on the edge of **Loch Scavaig**. It was named either from Helga Hollr (Norse for "Holy Hill") or after the warrior Aella who fought a fierce battle here against the Picts. The cafe at the top of the hill is renowned for its home baking. For a

The Cuillin from Elgol

souvenir with a difference, the shop here sells fishing floats, rescued from the beach and beautifully decorated by artist Hermione Lamond.

The road drops steeply to a tiny jetty. From Elgol, arguably, the definitive view of the Cuillin is to be found: It is from

Seals in Loch Scavaig

here that the Cuillin can be viewed from the south, looking directly into the horseshoe shaped ridge that encloses the mysterious **Loch Coruisk** which is separated from the sea by a narrow band of rock. A unique atmosphere, experienced by some with almost reverence, by others with a sense of foreboding, makes a trip to Loch Coruisk the highlight of a visit to Skye for many people. Loch Scavaig is known for its sudden squalls and storms due to the winds blowing down from the mountains

Loch Coruisk

but, weather permitting, boat trips are available from the jetty.

An alternative and exhilarating boat ride is available on the powerful rigid inflatable boat **Aquaexplore** which takes visitors to The Small Isles, with a chance to visit Kinloch Castle on Rum. This is a grand display of Edwardian opulence which was abandoned in its full glory, thus enabling one to literally "step back in time." Other destinations include the island of Soay where the remains of Gavin Maxwell's basking shark station can be seen.

The beach at Elgol is a wonderful place to spend some time. Overhanging sandstone cliffs have been sculpted by the wind and waves into strange formations. On a clear

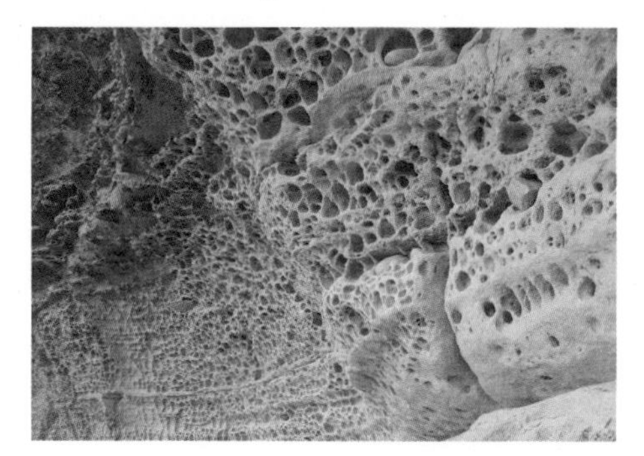

Weathered rocks, Elgol Beach

day it is possible to see Rum and Canna. A track leads north along the shoreline to **Camasunary** on the northern shore of Loch Scavaig. To the south of Elgol the headland contains many caves including **Prince Charles' Cave** where Bonnie Prince Charlie was hidden and protected by local residents until he could safely leave Skye for ever. As well as its royal connections, the cave is renowned for its collection of stalactites and stalagmites.

Glasnakille

From Elgol a small road runs to Glasnakille. It is well worth the drive here to enjoy the views across into the heart of Loch Eishort and to Ord, Tarskavaig Bay and the Point of Sleat at the southern tip of the Sleat Peninsula.

On a bleak headland sit the remains of **Dun Grugaig**, a well preserved early fortification. Also at Glasnakille is **Spar Cave**, also known in Gaelic as "Uamh Altriumin" – "Cave of The Nursing." Legend has it that an illegitimate child, born of the son and daughter of opposing clans, was kept here for safety until the child could be reclaimed. The cave is difficult to find and dangerous because of the tide so great care should be taken. Despite this, it was once a popular Victorian tourist attraction. Inside the cave was a pool surrounded by beautiful rock formations which had been sculpted by the water. Sadly, most of these were removed by early visitors and the cave lost much of its attraction

Sunset from Elgol

Public toilets can be found adjacent to the shop at the top of the hill at Elgol

4. MINGINISH -THE CUILLIN,, GLEN BRITTLE & LOCH HARPORT

Minginish is the area of central Skye north of The Cuillin and south of Loch Harport. Central Skye is dominated from all angles by the mighty Cuillin range whose rugged challenge attracts serious walkers and climbers from all over the World. The River Sligachan runs into Loch Sligachan north of the Cuillin. To the west is Glen Brittle and further to the north west is a beautiful corner which includes Talisker Bay and the western shore of Loch Harport. Minginish is characterised by a series of single track roads, each of which is an exciting journey of discovery and along which are several small craft workshops. To reach this beautiful corner, follow the A863 through Glen Drynoch and then take the B8009 (signposted Portnalong, Carbost and Talisker) which branches off to the south of Loch Harport.

The Red Cuillin

The A87 from Broadford clings to the shoreline along **Caolas Scalpay** (Caolas is Gaelic for "strait") between sea and mountains before reaching the head of **Loch Ainort** where a spectacular waterfall plunges beneath the road to join the loch. Names here are as dramatic as the scenery - the road makes the steep ascent below **Bruich nam Bò** ("Slope of The Cows") onto "The Ridge of Cloaks" beneath the twin peaks of **Beinn Dearg Mhor** (the Red Mountain) and Glamaig. The Red Cuillin are of a different rock from the gabbro of the Black Cuillin. They consist mainly of granite, which is paler in colour and has been eroded to much softer, rounded shapes. Glamaig, at 2543 feet (775m) is the highest point of the Red Cuillin.

Sconser

The nine hole golf course situated on the shore here is home to the **Isle of Skye Golf Club** and is imaginatively arranged with a variety of tee positions providing a different challenge second time around! For non-golfers, there is a gentle beach walk where the resident seals may be seen.

The **Sconser Lodge Hotel**, situated on the shore, was built in 1871 as a hunting lodge for the MacDonalds. The Seaview Dining Room, serving local produce, enjoys splendid views.

From Sconser, the Calmac ferry Loch Striven leaves for the fifteen minute crossing to the island of **Raasay**. (see section on Raasay.)

The Cuillin (The Cuchullins)

The Black Cuillin from the A863

The peaks of the Black Cuillin have been created from some of the World's oldest basalt and gabbro rock. They rise to form a seven mile long, horseshoe-shaped ridge of jagged peaks, the highest of which is **Sgurr Alasdair** at 3255 feet. Twelve of the Black Cuillin peaks are Munroes (over 3000 feet high.) Contained deep within the heart of the Cuillin, and separated from the sea by only a narrow rock bar, is atmospheric **Loch Coruisk**, which is only accessible by boat from Elgol or by a long and arduous walk.

Sligachan

Sligachan is best known as one of the main access points for the Cuillin: From here, paths and tracks lead off into the heart of the mountains. The path along the north shore of Loch Sligachan was once the main route to Portree. The "new" road was built by Telford in 1812, along with the beautiful stone, three-span bridge which crosses the river here. One legend, its origins unknown, advises people to dip their faces in the waters beneath the bridge to achieve eternal beauty! Above the road, towers the conical shaped mass of Glamaig.

Sitting at the head of Loch Sligachan is the family-owned **Sligachan Hotel**, well known to climbers for nearly one hundred and eighty years. In addition to a climbing museum, the hotel can boast unique beers brewed on site in **The Cuillin Brewery** and a selection of over two hundred malt whiskies to tempt the connoisseur. There is also a camp site, bunk house and mountain rescue post.

Sligachan is one of the main junctions on the island. The A87 continues north to Portree, while the A863 branches off to Dunvegan.

Public toilets available at first car park in Glen Brittle, at Glen Brittle camp site and by side of road in Carbost village (not always open.)

Glen Brittle
This lovely glen is bounded by The Black Cuillin and Glen Brittle Forest. The twin peaks of **Beinn a Bhràghad** and **Beinn Staic** rise above the mantle of trees. **Glen Brittle Forest** is criss-crossed by many tracks. Views of the Cuillin Ridge are truly magnificent from the road. The **River Brittle** is joined by several tributaries which meet the river in a series of rushing waterfalls. **Coire na Creiche Waterfalls** and **The Fairy Pools** are signposted from the second car park as the road descends into Glen Brittle proper. The mile or so between the car park and the falls slopes gently upwards but is not too strenuous a walk.

The road to Glen Brittle

The River Brittle joins **Loch Brittle** across a wide sandy beach. The western shores of the loch, like much of the Minguinish coastline, are steep and difficult to access. However, from the car park at the end of the road, paths follow the line of the eastern shore or take those more adventurous into the Cuillin. There is a hostel, a mountaineering hut, a mountain rescue post and a camp site. For the less mobile there are splendid views from the car park of the islands of Rum and Canna. Alternatively, a gentle walk can be taken along the path past Glen Brittle House, to **Eas Mor Waterfall** just over a mile away.

The Talisker Distillery, Carbost

Carbost
Carbost is the main settlement on the Minginish peninsula. In addition to various types of accommodation, there is a shop, pub, doctor and post office. Carbost is the home of the **Talisker Distillery**, presently the only distillery on Skye. There is a visitor centre offering tours of the distillery. Carbost is also a rendezvouz point in the annual Classic Malts Yacht Rally, when a large number of yachts anchor in the loch.
The Old Inn is a must! With log fires,

The Old Inn, Carbost

pub food, a patio right on the shores of the loch and even its own moorings, it is a place to relax and experience warm island hospitality. Impromptu music sessions are a regular occurrence.

The shores of **Loch Harport** are rich in wildlife. Otters and seals are regular

The head of Loch Harport from Carbost

visitors. Much smaller, and harder to spot, are sandhoppers or "beach flies." These tiny creatures, about a centimetre long, normally live just under the sand but come out to feed on the remains of dead animals. Oystercatchers and sandpipers find a plentiful supply of food among the

Minginish Tourist Route, Carbost

mussels, crabs and other smaller sea creatures. The shoreline is also rich in sea flora. Information boards in the parking and picnic area adjacent to the distillery give details of what to look out for on the seashore – a splendid place for the young and not-so-young to potter about.

Talisker Bay

The walk to Talisker Bay

The single track road which runs from Carbost through **Glen Oraid** affords views of the Outer Isles before arriving at Talisker Bay, which shelters between the two lofty headlands of **Rubha Cruinn** and **Talisker Point**.

Legend would have us believe that it was

Preshal More, Talisker

here that Cuchulainn stepped ashore from Ireland when he strode across the sea to become a pupil at Sgàthach's School for Heroes in the Cuillin. On the way he trod on the back of a fish thus causing the two "bruise" marks which can still seen on every haddock!

At the end of the road, nestling beneath the conical shaped mound of Preshal More, is the elegant Talisker House and gardens. The house dates from the early Eighteenth Century and was visited by the famous travellers Boswell and Johnson. It is currently available as holiday accommodation. It is possible from here to follow the signposted path to Fiskavaig. A quarter of an hour's walk beyond the house is a delightful beach with a mixture of both black and white sand as well as pebbles.

Portnalong

Portnalong's tiny harbour

Picturesque Portnalong is situated where **Loch Harport** joins **Loch Bracadale**. Local fishing boats operate from a small pier. Beyond is **Ardtrek Point** with its lighthouse. Families from overpopulated parts of Harris and Lewis were resettled in Portnalong after the First World War. They were given a piece of land to establish a croft from which, along with traditional weaving skills they had brought with them, they could make a living. A high class gallery, The **Loch Harport Gallery**, displays oils, water colours and sculptures by various artists.

Fiskavaig Bay

A tiny road winds its way from Portnalong to sleepy Fiskavaig Bay, renowned for its attractive blue shells,

Deserted buildings at Ardtrek above Fiskavaig Bay

magical sunsets and views of the islands of **Oronsay** and **Wiay** and beyond to MacLeods Tables. Golden Eagles fly here, as well as the area accommodating a remarkable number of smaller birds. In autumn large flocks of redwings gather in the trees, sporting their distinctive underwing red flash when disturbed. The pretty township of Fiscavaig has some highly individual craft studios as well as several bed and breakfast establishments for anyone wishing to linger. The area is popular for fishing, as it was in Norse times – Fiskavaig translates as "Bay of The Fish."

Glen Eynort

The **Eynort River**, flanked by reeds, meanders below spectacular mountains before emerging into **Loch Eynort**. Beyond the end of the road are the ruins of two churches and a cemetery. A Sixteenth Century font from the smaller and older of the two churches is now exhibited in an Edinburgh museum. Carved slabs can be seen in the ruins of the larger church.

From the tiny settlement of Eynort a nine mile circular walk through **Glen Brittle Forest** is signposted.

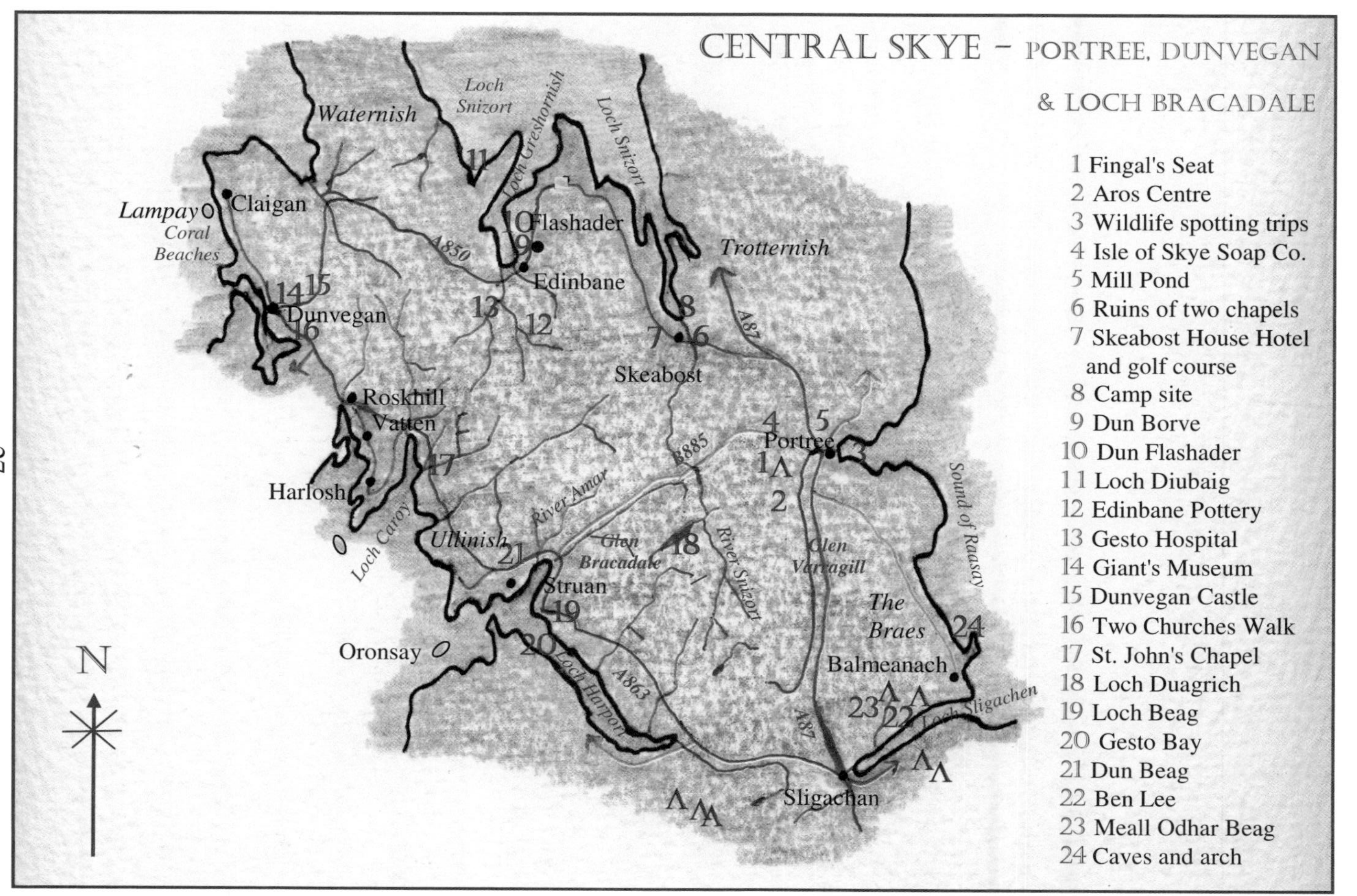
CENTRAL SKYE – PORTREE, DUNVEGAN
& LOCH BRACADALE
1 Fingal's Seat
2 Aros Centre
3 Wildlife spotting trips
4 Isle of Skye Soap Co.
5 Mill Pond
6 Ruins of two chapels
7 Skeabost House Hotel and golf course
8 Camp site
9 Dun Borve
10 Dun Flashader
11 Loch Diubaig
12 Edinbane Pottery
13 Gesto Hospital
14 Giant's Museum
15 Dunvegan Castle
16 Two Churches Walk
17 St. John's Chapel
18 Loch Duagrich
19 Loch Beag
20 Gesto Bay
21 Dun Beag
22 Ben Lee
23 Meall Odhar Beag
24 Caves and arch
Waternish
Loch Snizort
Loch Greshornish
Trotternish
Lampay
Claigan
Coral Beaches
Flashader
Edinbane
A850
Dunvegan
Skeabost
A87
Roskhill
Vatten
Harlosh
Loch Caroy
Portree
B885
River Amar
Ullinish
Glen Bracadale
River Snizort
Glen Varragill
Struan
The Braes
Sound of Raasay
Oronsay
Loch Harport
A863
Balmeanach
Loch Sligachen
Sligachan
N

5. CENTRAL SKYE - PORTREE, DUNVEGAN & LOCH BRACADALE

North of the Cuillin Hills much of central Skye is bleak moorland, crossed by few roads and the view broken only by areas of forestry commission land. However, the area is not without interest or beauty. The A87, A850 and A863 skirt the outer perimeter of the area with panoramic views of the many lochs which form deep indents into the landscape. To the north, the A850 curves around the shores of Loch Snizort Bheag and Loch Greshornish. Along the western side the A863 follows the length of Loch Bracadale and Loch Harport. To the east the A87 follows the coast through Portree and beyond.
The area can boast its own coral beach and has many historical sites, seeming to be positively littered with the ruins of brochs, duns and ancient chapels. A large number of these are relatively close to the road

Glen Varragill
From Sligachan, the A87 climbs steeply into Glen Varragill with panoramic views down the length of Loch Sligachan and beyond to the Isle of Raasay. Glen Varragill is a huge area of peat bogland with areas of forestry commission planting. The **Old Man of Storr** is visible beyond Portree in clear weather.

Braes
Signposted from the A87, a mile and a half south of Portree, Braes means "hillsides." Sheltering beneath the slopes of **Ben Lee** are several small settlements overlooking the Sound of Raasay. In 1882 this was the scene of "The Battle of Braes." As in Glendale, crofters rebelled against their impending eviction by their landlord.
The area is rich in wildlife, including corncrakes, and orchids thrive here. At **Balmeanach** the sandy beach is actually a tombola, a sandy bar which joins rocky An Aird to Skye. Caves and a natural arch can be found on the outer side of An Aird. (These are only accessible at low tide and great care should be taken.)

Portree
Situated two thirds of the way up the eastern coast of Skye, Portree is the island's administrative centre. Originally called Kiltaraglen, it was renamed Port an Righ (the King's harbour) in 1540 after James V visited the island. Dominated by the 1367' high Beinn na Greine, the town

Portree

stands above a natural harbour with views across to the isle of Raasay. Portree is a working port: fish are landed here and it is a popular stopping off place for visiting yachts and other tourist boats as well as being the home of the Portree Lifeboat. Wildlife spotting trips leave from the pier which was built by Thomas Telford in the 1820's. In earlier times, this was often the embarkation point for emigrants who had been evicted from their crofts. Nowadays there are shops, banks, hotels, a hospital, tourist information as well as the island's only

secondary school and all the other facilities one would expect to find in a small town.
The town is on two levels. The harbour is particularly captivating with brightly painted buildings. Once mainly warehouses, these now house a variety of pubs, restaurants and gift shops. A small shop at one end sells a wide selection of deliciously fresh, locally caught fish. The upper level of the town centres on **Somerled Square.** Handmade soap is produced at the **Isle of Skye Soap Company** Accessed from Hedgefield Road, a former mill pond has been converted by local school children into a conservation area where newts, frogs and toads have established themselves in large numbers.

The Aros Centre

The Aros Centre is a purpose built tourist facility with a cinema, frequent live entertainment, an audio visual presentation about Skye, indoor and outdoor play areas, an art gallery, a "nestcam" showing live pictures transmitted from within an eagle's nest, a cafe and a large gift shop. Admission to the main centre is free. Guided three hour tours of various parts of the island leave from here. From the Aros Centre a signposted Forest Enterprise walk climbs to **Fingal's Seat (Suidh Fhinn.)**

Skeabost

The **River Snizort**, the island's longest river, flows into **Loch Snizort Beag** at Skeabost. This was the setting for a fierce Sixteenth Century battle between the MacLeods and the MacDonalds, during which many clan members literally "lost their heads." A gruesome sight was the dismembered heads later to be seen floating down the river!

Skeabost was another place where St. Columba established a religious base. The remains of two chapels can be seen on an island in the mouth of the River Snizort which can be accessed via a footbridge adjacent to Skeabost Bridge. Some interesting tombstones can also be found in the undergrowth here.
On the edge of the loch is The **Skeabost House Hotel** with its nine hole golf course.

The Isle of Skye Trekking Centre

For those who like to enjoy the view from horseback, the Isle of Skye Trekking Centre is open all year and offers treks to suit all abilities, including beginners. It is situated about ten miles from Portree at Suladale on the A850.

Loch Greshornish

Loch Greshornish is one of the more secluded sea lochs of Skye. On its eastern shores, near **Flashader**, is a camp site. The remains of two ancient strongholds, **Dun Borve** and **Dun Flashader**, can also be seen. Down the western side a minor road runs to the **Greshornish House Hotel** which enjoys a spectacular setting. From here a track crosses the peninsula to the shores of **Loch Diubaig**, a remote and beautiful place. Nearby are the remains of two separate sets of hut circles and a prehistoric burial site.

Edinbane

Situated at the head of Loch Greshornish, Edinbane is now bypassed by the main road. Within the village are two hotels, a shop and **Edinbane Pottery** where it is possible to witness stylish and distinctive ceramics being created. A rather elegant but disused former hospital stands incongruously in the middle of Edinbane. This was the **Gesto Hospital**, built by

Kenneth McLeod. Having made his fortune away from the island as a tea planter, he returned to the area and provided the hospital for the benefit of local people.

Dunvegan

Dunvegan is situated at the head of Loch Dunvegan in the north west of the island. It is a popular place with a range of accommodation, several shops, a filling station, small bakery and a camp site. There is also a particularly helpful tourist information centre which incorporates an imaginatively stocked gift shop. Sea Eagles, Peregrines and Golden Eagles are regular visitors to this part of Skye and a board within the tourist information centre has an up to date list of which birds have been recently seen in the area. There is much to see and do in and around Dunvegan and there is a large car park in the middle of the village.

The St. Kilda Connection

This is a high class woollen shop selling Scottish knitwear and jewellery.

The Giant MacAskill Museum

Housed in a beautiful thatched cottage on the main road, this quirky museum is devoted to Giant Angus MacAskill. At 7'8" tall, he was reputedly the tallest Scotsman ever to have lived, although he did not actually live in Dunvegan – or even on Skye. His family were forced to emigrate from Harris to Cape Breton when Angus was only six years old. As he grew (and grew!) to manhood, he became famous throughout Canada. The museum was created by another member of the MacAskill Clan in memory of his kinsman and all others who were forced to leave their native Highlands and Islands. As well as having a serious side, this is a fun visit, and should certainly be on anyone's "not to miss" list.

Dunvegan Castle remains one of the oldest inhabited castles in the British Isles and has been the home of successive

Dunvegan Castle

MacLeod Chiefs for over seven hundred years. Within the castle can be viewed a famous relic - "**The Fairy Flag**" which is reputed to have magical qualities. Other fascinating artefacts include a locket containing a lock of Bonny Prince Charlie's hair and a pincushion belonging to Flora MacDonald on which she had embroidered the names of many of his supporters. The castle sits in beautiful

Dunvegan Castle Gardens

gardens, including a restored walled garden. Boat trips can be taken from the grounds to see the seal colony resident in

Loch Dunvegan. There is a gift shop in the castle as well as a large one across the road from the main gate. This is also where **MacLeod's Tables Restaurant** serves a wide range of wholesome food.

The Two Churches Walk

A leaflet, available from the tourist information centre, describes this circular (not very strenuous) walk which takes in two churches, a standing stone and the ruins of an old deserted village. This is a particularly pleasant way to spend a spare hour.

The Coral Beach

The Coral Beaches

Beyond Dunvegan Castle a minor road continues the three and half miles to **Claigan**. Near the end of the road is a car park from where a signposted path leads the mile or so to the coral beaches. Not

Shells and "Coral"

Berries and lichen near Claigan

true coral, the beach consists of the skeletal remains of a rare type of seaweed called Mael. It is a beautiful beach with the small uninhabited island of **Lampay** accessible at low tide. Claigan is also the site of a souterrain.

Loch Bracadale

(For Roag and Orbost, see the section on Duirinish.)

The A863 between Dunvegan and Bracadale is best travelled on a day when there is time to stop and explore, as there are several interesting detours from the main road. At **Roskhill** a minor road forms a loop round the peninsula where the townships of **Vatten** and **Harlosh** are

Croft house near Harlosh

to be found, flanked by Lochs Vatten and Caroy. The peninsula juts out into Loch

Bracadale. From the end of the road, beyond Harlosh, it is possible to walk to **Harlosh Point** where there is a cave and a stack with **Harlosh Island** beyond. On the western side of the headland are the remains of a chapel.

St. John's Chapel

St. John's Chapel

At the head of **Loch Caroy**, next to the A863 but hidden from the road apart from a small sign, are the ruins of St. John's Chapel and a graveyard which can only be described as breathtakingly beautiful. Care is needed to park off the road here. Through an archway a path meanders down between ancient crosses and tombstones, over which nature seems to have cast a magic spell: Branches of trees the have enfolded themselves protectively around the stonework and ferns have softened the stark outlines. At the bottom, where the graveyard almost meets the sea, there are some ancient Celtic crosses as well as a poignant reminder of a much more recent tragedy.

Celtic cross

Ullinish

Another "loop" detour, The Ullinish Peninsula near Struan is a wild and atmospheric place with views out into Loch Bracadale across the islands of **Oronsay**, **Wiay** and **Tarner**. There are striking views of the Cuillin Hills to the south east and MacLeods Tables to the north west. From the bottom part of the "loop" a lesser road leads towards the tip of the peninsula before becoming a track which continues to **Ullinish Point**. A tidal causeway connecting the island of Oronsay with The Point makes an exciting walk. (Great care should be taken not to undertake this when the tide is due to rise.)

At the imposing **Ullinish Lodge Hotel** it is possible to enjoy luxurious comfort and stunning cuisine whilst staying in the very room where Doctor Samuel Johnson slept during his Eighteenth Century tour of Scotland with his friend Boswell.

Dun Beag

Dun Beag

This Iron Age broch stands above the

A863 and, as it is only a short walk from the signposted picnic area by the roadside, it is one of the island's most accessible brochs. Much of the double walls can still be seen and in places remain to a height of about sixteen feet. Between the outer and inner walls are the remains of a flight of steps. The information boards here and at the car park are excellent. From the car park there are panoramic views over Loch Bracadale, to Ardtreck Point, the islands of Oronsay and Wiay in the foreground and Barra and South Uist in the distance.

Steps within the walls of Dun beag

Struan

Struan overlooks **Loch Bracadale** and **Loch Beag**. The village has a shop, outdoor clothing shop, garage, churches and a restaurant/bistro. There is also a pony trekking centre. The **Amar River** runs down nearby **Glen Bracadale** into Loch Beag. A track leads up the Glen to the beautiful and remote **Loch Duagrich**. On the eastern shore of Loch Beag, just off the road, are the grass covered remains of a broch, Dun Diarmaid

Public toilets available at Portree, in the main car park Dunvegan, and the car park for Dunvegan Castle.

Dun Diarmaid

Gesto Bay

Gesto Bay

A viewpoint near the side of the A863 affords splendid views over Gesto Bay and Loch Harport to the Black Cuillin. Half a mile from the viewpoint a minor road leads down to the bay and to the interesting ruins of an Eighteenth Century house.

Loch Harport

TROTTERNISH

1 Dun Gerashader
2 A Chorra-bheinn
3 Ben Dearg
4 Storrs Loch Power Station
5 The Old Man of Storr
6 Lealt Waterfall

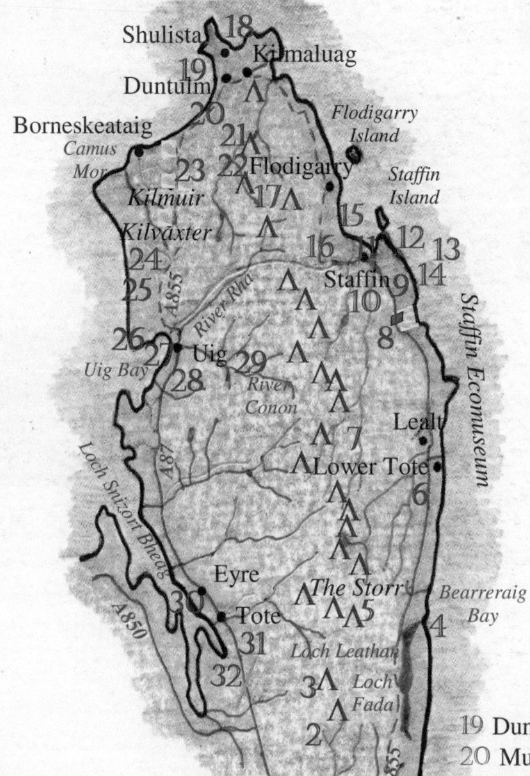

7 Loch Cuithir
8 Loch Mealt
9 Kilt Rock
10 Fossil Museum
11 Columba 1400
12 Staffin Slipway
13 Hut circles
14 Chambered cairn
15 Staffin Bay Cruises
16 Dun Beag
17 The Quiraing
18 St. Moluag's Chapel

19 Duntulm Castle
20 Museum of Island Life
21 Kilvaxter Souterrain
22 Kilmuir Old Graveyard
23 Breaton's Croft House
24 Eilean Chaluim Chille
25 Chambered cairn
26 Isle of Skye Brewery
27 Pottery
28 Captain Fraser's Folly
29 Fairy Glen
30 Standing stones
31 Chambered cairn
32 Pictish stone

6. TROTTERNISH

Trotternish is Skye's largest peninsula, its most northerly and possibly its most dramatic. Nature's power is grandly demonstrated in an awe-inspiring volcanic ridge which dominates the skyline almost two and a half thousand feet above the sea. It is a beautifully haunting place which is geologically unique. Once heavily forested, few wooded areas remain. The lower reaches of the ridge are flanked by vast tracts of peat moorland, across which flow countless rivers and streams which end abruptly, to plunge over the edge of towering sea cliffs.

The diverse range of terrain here provides habitats for a large number of bird species: Whinchats, twites, pipits, dunlins, greenshanks, golden plovers and the elusive corncrake can all be seen, as can buzzards, kestrels and Golden and White Tailed Eagles.

Dun Gerashader

About a mile north of Portree, above and to the right of the A855, are the remains of Dun Gerashader which is a stone fort dating from the Iron Age. The ruin is now much reduced in height but the outline can still be seen.

Loch Fada and Loch Leathan

Four miles north of Portree, beneath the towering peaks of **A Chorra-bheinn** and **Ben Dearg** sit pretty Lochs Fada and Leathan - now joined to form one loch. The car park half way along Loch Leathan is a lovely place to enjoy a flask of coffee or simply sit and savour the view. (A bus stop near the dam is convenient for exploring this area on foot.)

Storr Lochs Power Station

A tiny road leads from the end of Loch Leathan across a dam to two small car parks, near an observation platform overlooking huge pipes which run almost vertically to the shore four hundred feet below. Electricity had arrived on Skye in 1949, via a cable under the sea from Kyle, but from 1952 the island had its own hydro electric power station here. For several years all the island's power was generated at Storr Lochs but now demand is much greater so this power station is used only to supplement the National Grid in times of high demand.

Storrs Loch Power Station

From the viewpoint there are good views of the islands of Rasaay and Rona in the foreground and beyond to Applecross and Torridon on the mainland.

Bearreraig Bay

Bearreraig Bay

A steep path leads down to the beach from the power station car park. It is well worth the walk (and the climb up again!) This beautiful and secluded bay is rich in fossils dating back to the Jurassic period.

The Storr

The Storr

Powerful earth movements have pushed massive layers of rock skywards to produce this impressive ridge rising to almost two thousand four hundred feet above the sea. A single 165' high pinnacle, **The Old Man of Storr**, is visible for miles around like a giant finger pointing skywards. A path up the Storr to the Old Man leads from the roadside car park. One legend tells us that the Old Man and his wife (who fell down so is no longer beside him) were turned to stone because they had witnessed something no human should see.

Staffin Ecomuseum

Ecomuseum information board

Along the eastern coast of Trotternish, from the Storr to Flodigarry, a truly excellent series of information boards brings alive both past and present and transforms a thirteen mile stretch of coastline into one fascinating heritage trail. Geological features, archaeology, history and natural history are all here to discover.

Lealt Waterfalls

Near Lealt

Twelve miles north of Portree, near Lower Tote, the **River Lealt** has cut a deep gorge through which it plunges before dropping to the shore below in a spectacular waterfall.

Loch Cuithir

A track leads inland from Lealt for a walk of an hour and a half to **Loch Cuithir**. A curious association for what outwardly appears to be such a peaceful part of the world is the contribution made towards the production of dynamite! The track follows in part the route of an old railway line used to carry diatomite, a clay like substance which was formed from tiny ground up shells and which has a wide number of uses including the manufacture of dynamite. Diatomite was discovered in Loch Cuithir and extracted commercially from the beginning of the last century for a period of about fifteen years. The substance was transported to the shore where it was dried – the remains of the drying building can still be seen.

Loch Mealt

Loch Mealt is a pretty loch which passes underneath the road. A car park and picnic area provide the viewing point for where Loch Mealt spills over the two hundred and fifty feet high cliff to a shoreline of caves and arches, although many of these are inaccessible. From the viewpoint can be seen the stretch of coastline known as **Kilt Rock** where cliffs of basalt columns give the coastline a pleated appearance, hence the name.

Kilt Rock

Staffin Fossil Museum

At the road junction just beyond Loch Mealt stands Staffin Museum, housed in a reconstructed Nineteenth Century schoolhouse. Exhibits illustrate the geology and history of Trotternish and include dinosaur fossils which were found in the area.

Stafiin Fossil Museum

Staffin

Staffin & The Quiraing

The name Staffin comes from the Norse for "pillar." It is one of the larger settlements on Skye and nestles beneath the strangely shaped pinnacles of The Quiraing. The village overlooks the wide curve of Staffin Bay where the sea laps around the Isle of Flodigarry and Staffin Island before rolling onto a pebbled beach in an endless progression of frothy white waves. Staffin is a place where there are speckled houses, where dinosaurs once trod, where Stone Age people lived and where the circular foundations of Iron Age huts can still be seen. There are shops, a post office, a restaurant, a filling station and, at Columba 1400, a cafe and internet services. Take the scent of heather home with a perfumed candle from **Skyelight Candles.** Paths are signposted along the headland and shore. **Staffin Slipway** is not to be missed – a delightful area where some of the earliest inhabitants of Skye settled some 8500 years ago. Their circular wooden dwellings have long since gone but the raised circular foundations, known as **hut circles**, mark where these early houses once stood. A

chambered cairn is also to be found nearby. From an even earlier date, dinosaur footprints were discovered at Staffin Beach.

Across from the slipway is **Staffin Island** where upright poles remain from when fishermen used to dry their nets here.

Staffin Bay Cruises run an excellent hour and a half boat trip along the Trotternish coastline, from where it is possible to see many of the caves, natural arches and waterfalls which are not visible from the land. Alternatively, fishing trips can be pre-booked.

Near Staffin Slipway

The Quiraing

At the northern end of the Trotternish Ridge is The Quiraing, a collection of truly amazing rock formations including "**The Prison**" and "**The Needle**" and a huge flat plain in the centre of the peaks. This is "The Table" where cattle were once hidden from marauders. There are many tales of ghostly sightings in the Quiraing, including legendary giants who lived in a secret part of the rocks behind a huge keyhole-shaped opening. To truly appreciate the pinnacles of the Quiriang they should be approached on foot but, for the less energetic, a narrow road leading off to the west from Staffin, affords a closer view than from the A855. Also along this road are the ruins of **Dun Beag**, an Iron Age fortification.

Flodigarry

North of Staffin is Flodigarry, a township which was once the home of Flora MacDonald. She moved to Flodigarry when she married, four years after the Prince's escape. Her former home is now part of the **Flodigarry Country House Hotel** which enjoys a magnificent setting. **Flodigarry Island** lies just out to sea across a short stretch of water known as **Poldorais** ("the pool of Doras.") A way-marked path to the beach highlights points of interest. There is also a hostel with a camping area.

Kilmaluag

Kilmaluag is the most northerly part of Trotternish, also of Skye. There is a feeling of true remoteness here, of being on the top of the World. A minor road follows the Kilmaluag river north across the coastal plane to the ruins of **St. Moluag's Chapel**. St. Moluag is thought to have been a missionary who originated in Lismore. He established a monastery on the Isle of Raasay as well as several outlying chapels throughout the Hebrides, including the one at Kilmaluag. Near the rocky beach is a car park and picnic area.

By the main road is **The Trotternish Gallery** where an artistic husband and wife team paint beautiful Skye scenes.

At **Shulista,** Skye's first school was built in 1610.

Duntulm

Duntulm ("Fort on The Cliff") on the north western corner of Trotternish is a wild and awe inspiring place, a favourite haunt of Golden Eagles. On a clear day there are views across the Minch to the Shiant Islands. In the shadow of **Cnoc**

Roll is **Duntulm Castle**, precariously clinging to the top of cliffs which drop vertically to the sea. An Iron Age broch once stood here, later a Pictish Fort then a Norse stronghold and eventually a MacDonald castle. Legends give several possible explanations why they eventually abandoned the castle, one being that a careless nurse dropped a MacDonald baby from a window onto the rocks below. Wherever the truth lies, it takes little imagination to feel the presence of those who have passed this way in previous centuries. Perhaps it is the wish to leave ones own mark on history that has inspired the collection of strange stone sculptures which continue to develop close by. From Duntulm, the hills on the

Duntulm Castle

distant Isle of Harris can be seen across the Minch. Sunsets viewed from here are truly breathtaking.

Kilmuir

Gaelic for "Mary's Chapel," this is the area covering northern and western Trotternish. On a clear day there are views across to the Waternish Peninsula and the Ascrib Islands while, further away, are the Outer Isles. It is a fascinating part of Skye with the remains of several ancient structures.

Skye Museum of Island Life is housed in a collection of seven thatched cottages, some of which are laid out exactly as they would have been during the late Nineteenth Century. Others contain a selection of artefacts illustrating other aspects of the island's history. Kilmuir is also the last resting place of several well known characters. **Kilmuir Old Graveyard** is reached beyond the museum along the minor road to **Heribusta**. A large Celtic cross standing high above all the others marks the grave of Flora MacDonald. She died in March

Sunset near Duntulm

1790. Also to be found here are the graves of several MacArthurs, family pipers to the MacDonald Clan. An intriguing epitaph on one stone slab remains incomplete, finishing mid sentence. The accepted story is that the relative who had commissioned the stone was drowned and the mason would not complete the work because he was no longer assured of receiving payment. The renowned author Seton Gordon, who wrote extensively about the Highlands and Islands, also lies buried here. Another fascinating gravestone takes the form of a knight in armour.

Kilvaxter Souterrain

Signposted from the road is a car park for visiting the souterrain which is an underground tunnel, seventeen metres

The Museum of Island Life

long and dating from the Iron Age. Unlike burial chambers, it is thought that these were used as places to store perishable food and as refuge during raids. An information board explains what can be seen.

A mound in the centre of a large flat area between the sea and the A855 near Kilvaxter was once an island, **Eilean Chaluim Chille**, in the middle of a shallow loch. Saint Columba established a chapel here, which became an important part of early religious life on Skye. When the loch was drained to create new land for farming, the island was left literally "high and dry!"

To the west of Chaluim Chille is one of Skye's best preserved chambered cairns.

Borneskeataig

A minor road leaves the A855 at Kilvaxter and travels towards Bornesketaig, a detour worth taking. Unlike many such blackhouses which fell to ruin, **Beaton's Croft House** which dates from around 1880 remained occupied until 1980. It was then purchased by the National Trust who renovated the outside in contemporary style, the inside being converted to holiday accommodation. The coastline near Borneskeataig is pretty and of geological interest. The cliffs are made of basalt columns which on the shoreline have been eroded to form a hexagonal pavement. Large groups of fulmars nest amongst the cliffs. At **Camus Mòr** ("The Big Beach") is a small jetty and nearby are several arches and caves. The beach is popular with otters who can sometimes be seen playing among the rocks or fishing in the bay.

The **Whitewave Outdoor Centre,** south of Kilmuir on the Uig road, offers adventurous holidays and courses – sea kayaking, windsurfing and outdoor education. Bikes are also available for hire.

Uig

Uig, the Norse for "sheltered bay," is the main settlement on Trotternish. The village is surrounded on three sides by high ground and consequently the approach from any direction affords panoramic views of **Loch Snizort** and **Uig Bay**. It is a busy fishing port and ferry terminal, ferries departing from here for Harris and North Uist in the Outer Hebrides. Facilities at Uig include a bus station, petrol station, youth hostel and camp site. At the Post Office is a gift shop and small bakery. Uig is also the home of the **Isle of Skye Brewery** where it is possible to watch the beer being brewed and visit the gift shop for a fascinating array of souvenirs for the discerning beer fan. **Uig Pottery** produces a distinctive range of high class ceramics. **The Pub At The Pier** and **The Ferry Inn** are the village's two pubs, both serving food and the latter also offering accommodation. **The Uig Hotel**

Uig Bay

also offers a warm welcome and is dog friendly by prior arrangement! Additional accommodation is available at several guest houses and B and Bs. Pony Trekking and bike hire are available in the area.

Captain Fraser's Folly is the name of the round tower on the southern side of the bay. Built on a whim, with no particular purpose, it dates from the mid 1800's.

Corncrakes can sometimes be seen (more often just heard!) in the surrounding area. Golden Eagles also frequent these parts and the rare White Tailed Eagle can sometimes be spotted from the headlands.

Waterfalls and The Fairy Glen

A series of pretty glens converge on Uig and there are many dramatic waterfalls in the area. From the Staffin road a path follows the **River Rha** upstream to where a double waterfall cascades into a shady pool. There are also falls on the **River Conan** which flows down Glen Uig. Here can be found "Fairy Glen," a magical miniature landscape crafted by the erosive powers of the river. There are strange conical hills, caves, a small loch and peculiar rock formations including **Castle Ewen** which is supposedly a fairy castle.

Loch Snizort

South of Uig the A87 follows the eastern shore of Loch Snizort. This is Skye's largest loch. It runs twelve miles inland from Waternish point, separating Trotternish and Waternish. St. Columba is said to have landed here. Later it was one of the places where Bonnie Prince Charlie sought shelter. The **River Snizort**, which is Skye's longest river, runs into the narrow southern arm of the loch known as **Loch Snizort Bheag** ("small Snizort.") The remains of ancient cairns and duns here are reminders of earlier settlers.

Kensaleyre Standing Stones

At Eyre (Gaelic for "gravel shore,") overlooking where **Loch Eyre** joins Loch Snizort Beag, two standing stones can be seen from the A87. Legend has it that these were placed there by a feine (a stone throwing giant) who would suspend his huge cooking pot over a fire between the two stones.

Also close to Kensaleyre, at the head of Loch Eyre, is a large chambered burial cairn.

Tote Pictish Stone

South of Kensaleyre, a minor road leads from the B8036 towards Tote where a Pictish stone dating from approximately two thousand years ago can be found. A small wooden enclosure surrounds the stone, which was erected here after being rescued from use as a doorstep during the Nineteenth Century!

There are public toilets in Portree, opposite the Museum of Island Life near Kilmuir and at Uig Ferry Terminal

7. WATERNISH

Situated between Skye's other two northern peninsulas, Waternish is the smallest of the three and is quite distinct from anywhere else on Skye. Meaning "watery point," Waternish is separated from Duirinish by Loch Dunvegan and from Trotternish by Loch Snizort and is a narrow strip of land eight miles long and a little over three miles wide. It is a place of majestic cliffs, rocky headlands and fast flowing streams which tumble down narrow gorges before cascading over the cliffs in spectacular waterfalls. Where the sea meets the shore, more benignly there are rocky beaches and gentle bays to explore.

A ridge of high land down the centre of the peninsula divides east from west, the highest points being Beinn Chreagach at 1069' and Beinn a Sgumain at 977'. To the west are Ardmore Point, Dunvegan Head and Isay Island. To the east are the Ascrib Islands, while further away looms the ridge of mountains running the length of Trotternish.

The settlements on Waternish were traditionally crofting communities; nowadays this is more true of the eastern half than the west which has seen the development of a wide variety of art and crafts enterprises with small studios and galleries dotted about. It is easy to understand why so many people have found inspiration here.

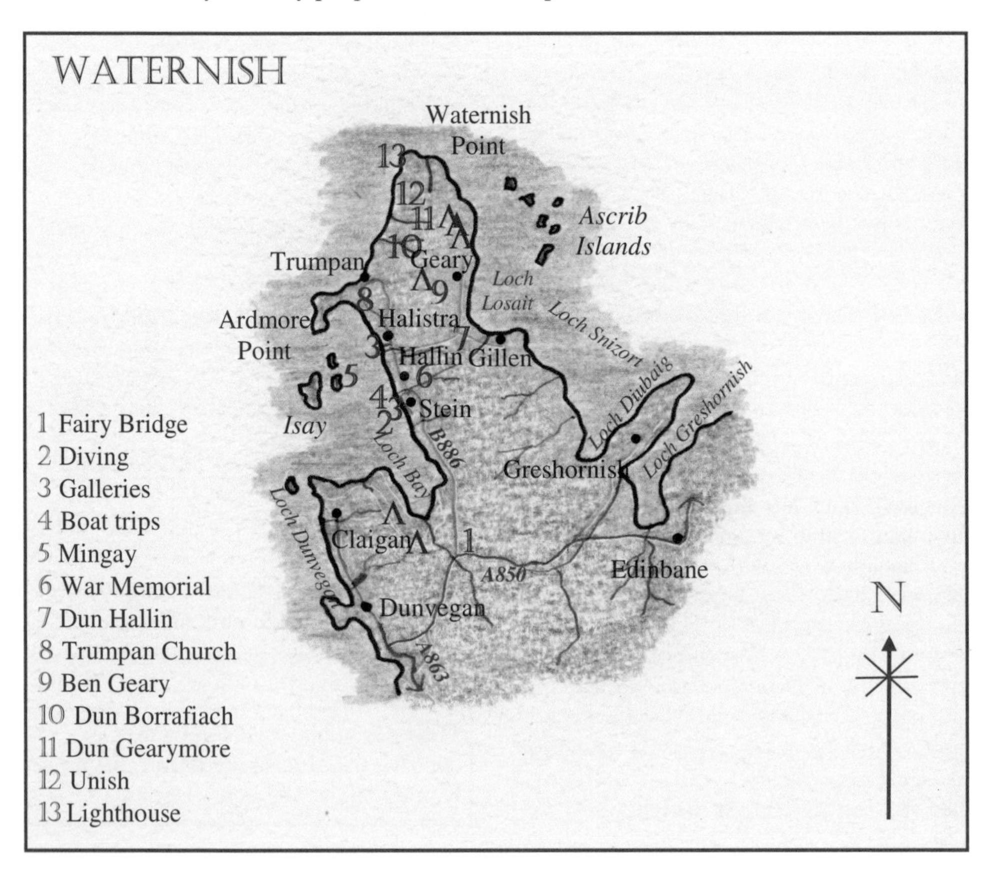

Waternish is steeped in history and has several ancient sites, ranging from two Iron Age brochs and several hut circles to a deserted village, the oldest inn on Skye, a historic purpose-built fishing village, a fairy bridge and an old church with a black and tragic history.
An abundance of wildlife enjoys the varied habitats here. Golden Eagles and buzzards soar overhead; seals, dolphins, otters and basking sharks swim close to the shores and the towering headlands are home to a myriad of sea birds including the Great Skua.
Unlike many parts of Skye, the population on the Waternish Peninsula is increasing. Over recent years there has been an influx of artists and craft workers and there are numerous small studios throughout the peninsula. It is well worth detouring along the several tiny roads for it is here where most of the small workshops and craft outlets are to be found.
Waternish is a place of endless sky and ever changing light and colour, somewhere to expect the unexpected and definitely a place to linger.

Fairy Bridge

Fairy Bridge
Where the B886 leads off towards Waternish is the Fairy Bridge. It was here, supposedly, that the fairy wife of a Macleod chief left him to return to her own people after a marriage of a year and day, which was all that the Fairy King would allow. She left behind both husband and child. The acclaimed "fairy flag" of Dunvegan Castle was reputed to have been a parting gift to her husband.
Beyond the Fairy Bridge a minor road leads down to the shore where the **Bay River** joins the loch across a pretty beach.

Stein
Stein is a small, very picturesque village designed by Thomas Telford. The village was planned in the late Eighteenth Century by The British Fisheries Society who provided the pier, the boats and even the nets for the community to establish itself. However, the venture was not a huge success and people began to move away in search of other employment. Happily, the village now thrives again as a tourist destination and home to several private enterprises. Whitewashed fishing cottages stretch along the waterfront. Loch Bay House, at the head of the road down into Stein, was once owned by rock star Donovan.

The waterfront at Stein

The Stein Inn, dating from 1790 and Skye's oldest inn, is full of character and offers accommodation as well as superb home cooked food, much of which is sourced locally. The inn also has four private moorings for yachting visitors. (A tidal slipway makes getting ashore easy!)

The pretty "main street" at Stein

Just along the road is the **Loch Bay Seafood Restaurant** which is nationally renowned for local crab, lobster and other freshly caught sea-food. Also on the waterfront is The Captain's House, home of **Dandelion Designs** – an unusual craft gallery and gift shop which specialises in pyrography, creating beautiful wooden clocks, plaques, breadboards etc. **Boat trips** are available from Stein during the summer. The sheltered waters of Loch Bay make this the ideal location for diving. Courses to suit all abilities are arranged by **Dive and Sea the Hebrides.** Up the hill from the village lies **Skyeskyns**, where sheep skins are cured and leather made. Next door is the **Brae Fasach** ceramics and painting studio.

SkyeSkyns

War Memorial

The Waternish War Memorial is situated to the right above the road leading to Hallin and occupies a particularly spectacular position with views out over Loch Bay and the islands of **Isay, Mingay** and **Clett** and beyond to Dunvegan Head.

Halistra

Halistra is primarily a crofting settlement. From Lower Halistra a narrow road branches off towards the sea. Down this road are some splendid small craft studios, including **Halistra Pottery** and **The Skye Yarn Company**.

Dun Hallin

Above Hallin are Dun Hallin and the remains of an Iron Age broch.

Ardmore Point

Beyond the settlement of Halistra, the road forks to the left long the headland overlooking lovely **Ardmore Bay,** which shelters behind Ardmore Point. From the

Ardmore

road there are good views of the islands of Mingay and Isay, while in the distance the hills of Harris and North Uist are visible on a clear day.

Trumpan

At Trumpan is a small car park and picnic site, with an information board and views to the Outer Isles. Across the road are an old graveyard and the ruins of **Trumpan Church** which was the scene of a bloody massacre, one of two to take place on a single day in 1578.

MacLeod worshippers were at prayer when MacDonald raiders from Uist set fire to the church and the congregation perished. The Macleod chief, on hearing about this atrocity, gathered reinforcements and unfurled the famous fairy flag. In Ardmore Bay the MacDonalds were too late to make their getaway. Their boats were captured and every MacDonald killed. Their bodies were buried beneath a dyke and the battle subsequently became known as **The Battle of The Spoiling of The Dyke.** In the church yard is the gravestone of Lady Grange, a sad lady who was incarcerated for many years by her husband after she threatened to disclose a Jacobite plot she had overhead. Also in the churchyard is

Trumpan Graveyard

The Trial Stone: Accused of a crime, a blindfolded person who could put their finger straight through a hole in the stone was deemed to be innocent. If this was not achieved first time the person was concluded to be guilty!

The headland near the church is a favourite haunt of wild geese. It is also one of the rare places where the shy corncrake bird may be spotted amongst the grass.

Waternish Point

The road does not go as far as the headland but a track continues for two and a half miles or so from a bend in the road half a mile from the car park. Along the way are a cairn in memory of a man who died in one of the many battles between MacLeods and MacDonalds, the remains of two Iron Age brochs (**Dun Borrafiach** and **Dun Gearymore**) and some hut circles. The track dwindles out at the ruins of the abandoned village of **Unish** but it is possible to continue the further mile to the lighthouse.

Geary and Gillen

Nestling beneath **Ben Geary**, the eastern and less visited side of the Waternish Peninsula is more of a traditional crofting community: To go there is to step back in time. Overlooking **Loch Snizort,** many of the crofting cottages remain much as they have been for many years. Hut circles to be found nearby on two separate sites are evidence of earlier settlements. **The Ascib Islands** look almost near enough to touch and on a clear day there are views of Trotternish and the mountains of The Storr to the north. Below Gillen lies the sweeping bay. of picturesque **Loch Losait**.

There are public toilets at Dunvegan.

8. DUIRINISH

Duirinish is Skye's most westerly peninsula, parts of which are inaccessible to all but determined walkers. It is edged by cliffs towering high above the sea which has sculpted fantastic caves, arches and stacks where large numbers of sea birds nest. The centre of the peninsula consists almost entirely of bleak moorland and steep slopes, dissected by fast flowing streams and deep glens which provide a welcoming habitat for buzzards, golden eagles, merlins and kestrels. At the southern tip is Idrigill Point, near which are three sea stacks known as MacLeod's Maidens. Visible from every angle are the twin, flat topped hills known as MacLeod's Tables, which stand at the heart of this remote and wild land. These are Healabhal Mhor and Healabhal Bheag. The flat tops of the mountains were supposedly created when the local chief failed to offer hospitality to Saint Columba. During a sermon (on hospitality!) the tops of the mountains were struck off to create a bed and a table for the saint. Healabhal Mhor stands over 1500' high while Healabhal Beag is just over 1600'. It is claimed that MacLeod chiefs would entertain guests by having lavish meals transported to the top of Healabhal Mor and then dining by torchlight.
The Hamara River flows south east to north west down Glen Dale, which forms the most hospitable part of the peninsula. The narrow roads which lead off from the B884 are well worth exploring to discover all manner of delightful places. (Glendale is the name given to this area rather than to one settlement.)

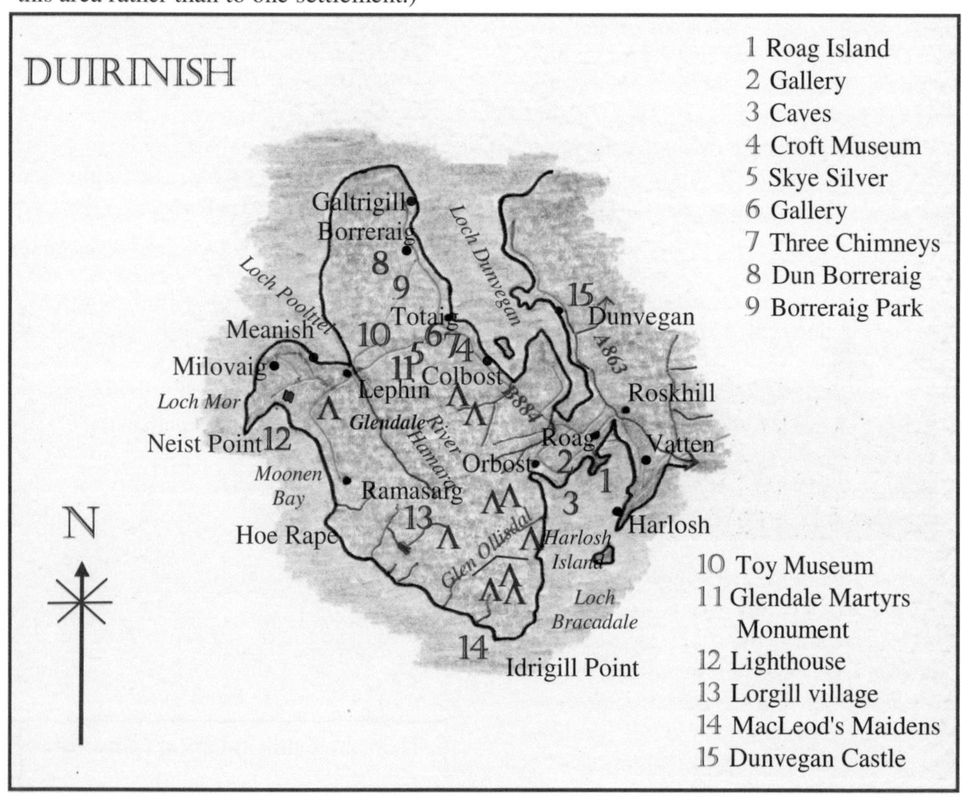

Roag

Roag Island

From the A863 at **Roskhill,** an unclassified road forms a loop to the small township of Roag, past picturesque **Roag Island a**nd beyond to Orbost before rejoining the main road. Roag is famous for its winkles. A tranquil place, it is difficult to believe that it was named "The Noisy Place" by the Norse and that King Haakon's defeated fleet sought refuge here in 1263.

Orbost Gallery

Open between April and October, this is one of Skye's many small galleries exhibiting top class art work. Stunning watercolours by Marion Roberts are exhibited alongside Paul Kershaw's evocative wood engravings and work by various other artists. This gallery really is a gem!

Orbost

Originally owned by the MacDonalds, the 4500 acre Orbost Estate was purchased in 1997 by Highlands and Islands Enterprise with the intention of creating smallholdings as an experiment in planned rural development. For various reasons, the plan has not yet come to full fruition.

There is a limited amount of parking near Orbost Farm, from where a number of walks are signposted along the track which leads beyond the farm. **Orbost House** was once home to authoress Otta Swire (1898 – 1973) who wrote about the legends and folklore of Skye. The track leads to a rocky beach where edible mussels can be found and where one can walk along the shore to the caves at **Meall Greepa**. Alternatively, from the track it is a five mile walk to **Idrigill Point** and then ten miles north west towards the deserted village of **Ramasaig.**

Walks from Orbost

Loch Dunvegan

Loch Dunvegan is a sea loch, an inlet of The Minch which separates Skye from the Outer Hebrides. The many rocks and skerries make it a favourite haunt for a large colony of seals. Seal viewing boat trips leave from the landing stage at Dunvegan Castle.

Colbost

Colbost still is a crofting community but the delightful **Colbost Croft Museum** demonstrates everyday life as it was during the Nineteenth Century. A reconstructed thatched blackhouse, complete with peat fire burning in the centre of the living quarters, gives visitors the chance to step back into the past. An illicit still would have been quite common near such a house and a replica is found here too.

Colbost is also home to **The Three**

Chimneys restaurant. Established in the 1980's, this has been acknowledged as one of the World's top restaurants. One of its signature dishes is Marmalade Pudding, the marmalade being home made on the premises.

Colbost Croft Museum

The Old School at Colbost now houses **Skye Silver,** jewellers with a difference. In addition to traditional Celtic designs, jewellery casts have been made from natural shapes such as tiny sea shells and coral from the nearby coral beach. In this way, nature's forms are reproduced in silver and gold. At **The Raven Press Gallery** artist Kathleen Lindsley produces wonderful prints from wood engravings, minute detail being carved in wood before being transferred to paper by block printing.

Borreraig

Beyond Colbost an unclassified road branches off the B884 to Borreraig. A signpost for Husabost leads to the gallery of artist Diana Mackie, renowned for capturing the elusive qualities of light. Returning to the Borreraig road, the remains of an Iron Age fortification, **Dun Borreraig**, perch on a rocky crag to the east of the road. It was at Borreraig that the renowned MacCrimmon family set up a college of piping which existed for over two hundred years and became famous throughout the World. Students studied for seven years before being considered proficient. A cairn commemorates the MacCrimmons' contribution to Scottish culture. A Piping Museum (still shown on maps) has been incorporated into the Borreraig Park Museum.

The road ends at **Galtrigill**, the remains of a village deserted in the 1950's and not one of the Clearance villages as is sometimes thought. Near here the **Manners Stone** was once to be found – people were reputed to find their manners if they walked three times around the stone. However, there are so many large stones here and several different stories about the stone being removed or broken up that it is impossible to find nowadays, even though it does remain marked on Ordnance Survey maps!

Borreraig Park Museum

Borreraig Park Museum

Along the road which cuts across Duirinish from Borreraig to Glendale is Borreraig Park, a small privately owned museum and craft shop which incorporates exhibits from the former piping museum. There is a extensive and fascinating collection of domestic bygones from the island as well as a history of the World famous McCrimmon pipers and a gift shop which could rival Aladdin's cave: In addition to postcards, books, CDs, jewellery and local crafts, there is a large selection of wool, tartan fabric, piping accessories, chanter kits (for the aspiring piper) and stunning knitwear produced on the premises. Open all year round, this is definitely one for the "must visit" list!

A gift shop to rival Aladdin's Cave !

Glendale Toy Museum

Toys are made to be played with - a philosophy which makes a visit here enchanting. Specialising in toys and games from the 60's, 70's and 80's, there are a large number of exhibits with which

Glendale Toy Museum

visitors are free to play. The museum is clearly signposted.

Loch Poolteil

The River Hamara flows into Loch Poolteil, where the massive height of **Dunvegan Head** provides some shelter in northerlies for the pier at **Meanish**. Only fishing boats and the occasional dive boat leave from here nowadays but this was once an important landing place: Until a proper road to Duirinish was built, supplies for this part of the island had to be brought in by boat. Seals and otters can often be seen as well as different birds of prey that live largely undisturbed in this remote area. Along the shore are rock pools containing beautifully coloured sea anemones.

Lephin

There is a food store and post office just off the B884 in Lephin.

The Glendale Martyrs

Glendale is still largely a crofting community but its tranquillity belies a turbulent history. Nineteenth Century inhabitants lived under the harsh regime of a landowner who wished to clear the glen to rear sheep. In 1882 the crofters met to make a stand against this injustice. A gunboat was sent to Glendale to quash the rebellion and the ringleaders were imprisoned in Edinburgh and later became known as the "Glendale Martyrs." A monument to their brave stance can be found beside the B884. Far from subduing the crofters, their resolve was strengthened. The whole question of

Martyrs' Monument

Clearances was brought into the open and in 1904 the Glendale crofters became the first to own their land. Security of tenure for crofters throughout Scotland followed.

Moonen Bay

Moonen Bay

The west coast of Duirinish is high, remote and largely unpopulated. From Neist Point in the north to Idrigill Point at the southern tip, cliffs rise a thousand feet above the sea. Moonen Bay stretches between the spectacular headlands of **Waterstein Head** and **Hoe Rape**. Here author Gavin Maxwell once fished for basking sharks.

Ramasaig

A waterfall tumbles onto the beach at remote Ramasaig Bay. High above the bay is the deserted village of Ramasaig, once a farming community but cleared around 1830. Signposted from Glendale, the ruins of the village can be reached by following the single track road which continues from the B884 at Hamaraverin. Just less than two miles beyond Ramasaig is **Lorgill**. The unfortunate inhabitants of this township were ordered to embark for Nova Scotia. Anyone too old to travel or without relatives to care for them was taken to the poor house. The ruins of over twenty dwellings still remain beside the Lorgill River.

Neist Point

To the west of Glendale are picturesque **Loch Mor** and the most westerly tip of Skye, Neist Point. Saxifrage and other

The lighthouse at Neist Point

tiny alpine plants cling to imposing cliffs of basalt columns creating a spectacular setting for the splendid Neist Point Lighthouse. At the end of the road is a car park, from which there is a steep path down to the lighthouse. The rocky beach near the lighthouse is full of imaginatively piled towers of stone, to which visitors continually add. The cliffs of **Waterstein Head** across **Moonen Bay**

Rock sculptures at Neist Point

from here are some of the highest in Europe and are truly awe inspiring.

9. RAASAY

The island of Raasay, 13 miles long and in places less than a mile wide, is a fifteen minute ferry journey from Sconser on Skye. Covering some sixty square miles of forest, moor, lochs, bog and rocky coastline, the island is a nature conservancy area and has a magical feel as somewhere quite distinct from anywhere else. Many people leave their vehicle at Sconser and take the ferry across for the day but anyone with time to spare should consider a longer visit, either with car or bicycle for there are many fascinating parts of the island to explore. (If taking a vehicle across, please note there is no filling station on the island.)

Raasay, like many parts of Skye, has suffered a somewhat turbulent history. For several centuries it was a stronghold of the MacLeods. Bonnie Prince Charlie was rowed to Raasay in the dead of night. He was hidden in a shepherd's hut but Raasay paid dearly for this act of loyalty to the Stuarts: Government troops laid waste to the island, leaving virtually nothing untouched and including the razing to the ground of the original Raasay House which was the Macleods' home. The MacLeod Laird spent most of his fortune trying to rebuild all that had been destroyed but he went bankrupt.

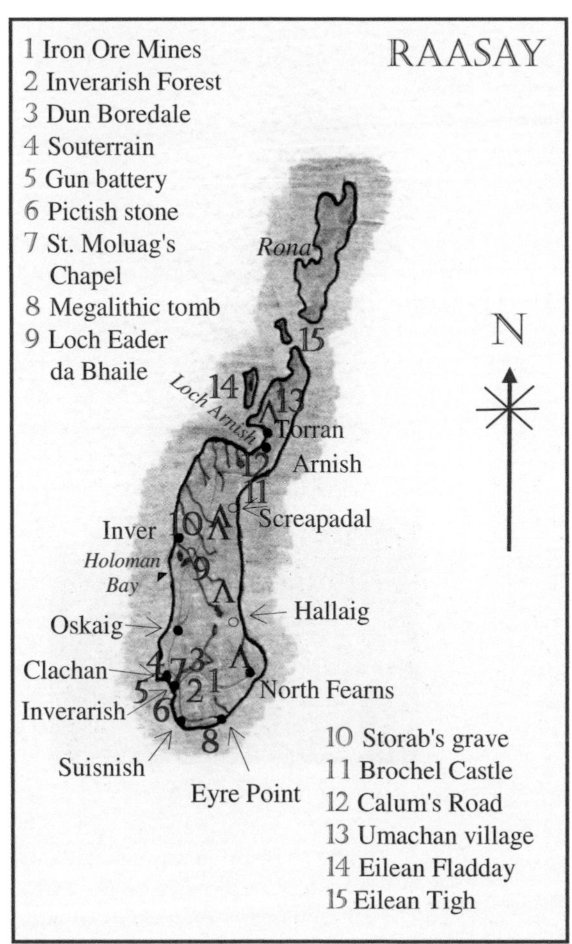

The population increased until the Clearances when many families were forced to leave. The island suffered mixed fortunes during the Twentieth Century. Less than two hundred people currently live on the island, nearly all in the southern part, but it is once again a thriving community with people employed in crofting, fish farming and tourism.

There are public toilets at the Sconser ferry terminal and also at Suisnish.

MV Loch Striven

The Iron Ore Mines
Industrial remains from a former iron ore mining industry litter the hill behind Suisnish. By following the line of the dismantled railway it is possible to walk up to the disused mine where there is now a picnic area with splendid views. The path became known as **"The Burma Road"** because the railway line was built by prisoners of war.

Former Iron Ore workings

Inverarish
This is the main village on Raasay and was largely built by First World War German prisoners who worked at the iron mine. Inverarish Terrace is a row of pretty white cottages which once housed the POWs. There is an extremely well stocked shop and post office with internet access, a public telephone, two churches, and a variety of B and B accommodation. Behind the village is **Inverarish Forest** with several marked woodland trails. Raasay has the distinction of having its own subspecies of vole, not found anywhere else.

Clachan
At Clachan is the **Borodale House Hotel** (formerly the Isle of Raasay Hotel.) The bar and restaurant are open to non residents. Permits for brown trout fishing from the lochs and lochans are available from the hotel. On the hill behind the hotel is **Dun Boredale**, an Iron Age broch. Near the old pier are the remains of a 2000 year old **souterrain**
Also overlooking Churchton Bay is **Raasay House**, an outdoor centre with cafe, accommodation and other facilities. Unfortunately this beautiful, newly refurbished Georgian building was all but destroyed by fire in early 2009 but is to be rebuilt. Behind Raasay House the **walled garden** is one of Scotland's oldest and is being lovingly brought back to its former glory. The grounds of Raasay House, which slope gently down to a small harbour, are rich in archaeological

St. Moluag's Chapel

interest. Near the harbour are the remains of a gun battery, a circular construction from the Napoleonic War. Built around

1810, it is decorated with two rather weather-beaten mermaids. Nearby, a **Pictish Stone** cut into the rock bears a unique cross design. A further similar freestanding stone can be seen nearby at the entrance to the forest. In the woods are the remains of another of **St. Moluag's chapels**. The forest is dotted with interest and an excellent Forestry Commission leaflet gives details of the various walks and things to be seen along the way.

The Stable Block

The stable block of Raasay house is a beautiful building. The clock in the tower stopped in 1914 when thirty-six Raasay men went away to war. Only fourteen came home.

The Stable Block

Oskaig

Two roads head north from Inverarish before joining some two and a half miles further north. The lower road passes through the hamlet of Oskaig, famous for being the birthplace of renowned Gaelic poet Sorley MacLean. From the rocky shoreline here there are good views across the Sound of Raasay to Skye. Beyond Oskaig is sweeping **Holoman Bay,** bounded by Oskaig and **Holoman Island** which is accessible at low tide, a fact the local sheep sometimes take advantage of.

Holoman Island

Dun Caan

By the road above **Loch Eader da Bhaile** is a car park from where the path starts for the ascent of Dun Caan, the flat top of an extinct volcano. At nearly 1500' high it is the highest point on the island and clearly recognisable from all around. The views of the Cuillin and, in the other direction, to Torridon are impressive. Legend has it that when Boswell, the famous Eighteenth Century traveller, visited Raasay he was so enthralled to be entertained to a meal on top of Dun Caan that he felt moved to dance an impromptu jig!

Inver

Beyond the lochs to the left of the road, a signposted path sets out for Inver. Near the start of the path is a cairn known as **Storab's Grave**. Storab was a Viking prince who was shipwrecked off Raasay. The islanders were afraid of him and killed him. Some flute music, inspired by the tale of Storab was written by a composer who lived on Raasay for a while. The walk continues through woods before emerging on the beach at Inver, a place where White Tailed Eagles are sometimes seen.

Screapadal

The road crosses over to the eastern side of the island towards another of Raasay's forests. There is a small parking area across the road from which a signed track leads south to the cleared township of Screapadal. Here, the remains of the settlement can still be seen.

Brochel Castle

A path leads from the roadside to Brochel Castle which perches precariously on the cliff top. Although in a dangerous state of ruin, it is still imposing and must have been an impregnable stronghold. It was built in the Fifteenth Century and was once the headquarters of Calum Garbh, son of the Ninth Chief of Lewis who, apparently, ran a profitable business in piracy! The castle was last inhabited at the end of the Seventeenth Century.

Brochel Castle

Callum's Road

The final two miles of road to Arnish are known as "Callum's Road" for they were built single handedly by Callum MacLeod. This was a magnificent feat by a determined and remarkable man. As well as unofficial road builder, he was also the postman and a relief lighthouse keeper for the light on the nearby island of **Rona**. Around 1900, Arnish was a community of around a hundred people, with a school just beyond at Torran. Over the years the village gradually declined. The lack of a proper road was one of the reasons and Callum repeatedly asked the council to provide one. When this was not forthcoming he set to and built it himself. It was a herculean task, involving felling trees, digging by hand, building culverts and moving huge

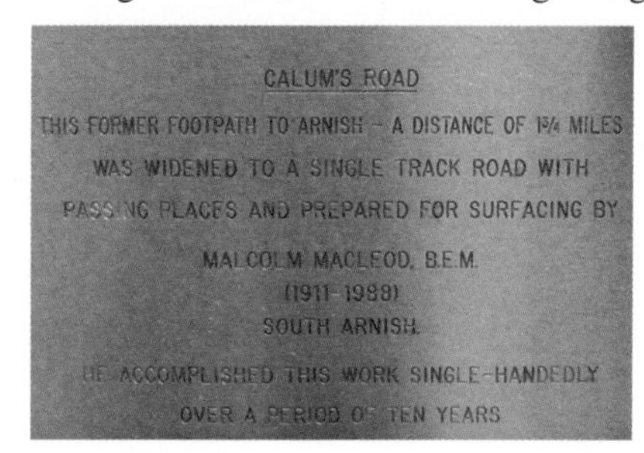

Part of the plaque to Callum MacLeod

amounts of earth but he never gave up. It took nearly ten years to complete and in the process he is said to have worn out tens of pairs of boots and nearly a dozen wheelbarrows before the road was finally "opened" in 1974. Sadly, by this time all the remaining families had moved away from Arnish. Callum continued to live there with his wife and maintain the road until his death in 1988. In 2006 a book entitled "Callum's Road" was written by Raasay author, Roger Hutchinson.

Arnish

The road ends at Arnish. This pretty spot abounds in banks of primroses and other wild flowers in the spring. There are wonderful views across the **Sound of Raasay** to Skye. Half a mile beyond the road is the old schoolhouse, now providing excellent holiday accommodation. From here a well trodden path follows the shoreline of **Loch Arnish** where **Eilean Fladday** is accessible at low tide across a natural

The end of the road

causeway. The four remaining miles lead to Raasay's most northerly point, off which lies **Eilean Tigh**. This, too, is accessible at low tide. A small bothy for walkers is situated near the northern tip of Raasay.

Loch Arnish

After skirting **Meall Dearg** a short path heads east towards the coast to **Umachin**, another ruined village.

Hallaig

The eastern side of Raasay is uninhabited and the only road is in the south from Inverarish to a car park at **North Fearns**. From North Fearns are incomparable views of Skye, Scalpay, the Crowlin Islands and Applecross on the mainland. From the car park a track leads northwards to Hallaig, possibly the most well known clearance village because of Sorley MacLean's evocative poem. The shore below Hallaig is a good place for finding fossils.

Eyre Point

From Iverarish a road follows the southern shore of Raasay, past Suisnish to Eyre Point which has a shingle beach overlooked by a modern, automated box type lighthouse. Nearby is a **dolmen** – a megalithic tomb in the form of three rocks supporting a fourth flatter one. Originally this would probably have been covered in small stones and earth to form a barrow.

Peat Digging

Peat is still widely used as a fuel throughout the highlands and islands. It consists of compressed, partially decayed vegetable matter and develops in boggy areas. Stacks of peat can sometimes be seen drying. Raasay is an area where, because of the large tracts of boggy land, peat is found extensively.

Peat digging

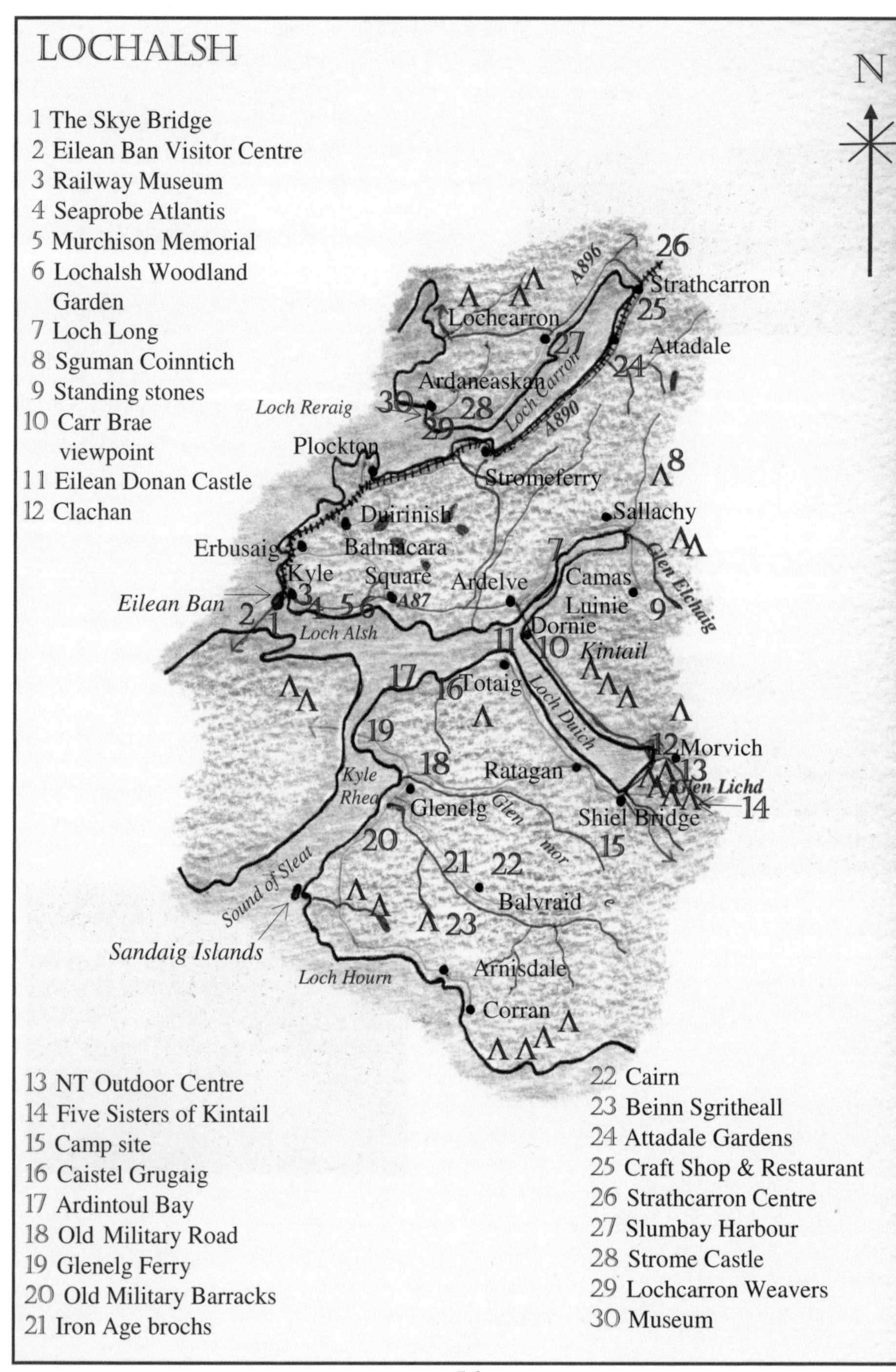
LOCHALSH
N
1 The Skye Bridge
2 Eilean Ban Visitor Centre
3 Railway Museum
4 Seaprobe Atlantis
5 Murchison Memorial
6 Lochalsh Woodland Garden
7 Loch Long
8 Sguman Coinntich
9 Standing stones
10 Carr Brae viewpoint
11 Eilean Donan Castle
12 Clachan
13 NT Outdoor Centre
14 Five Sisters of Kintail
15 Camp site
16 Caistel Grugaig
17 Ardintoul Bay
18 Old Military Road
19 Glenelg Ferry
20 Old Military Barracks
21 Iron Age brochs
22 Cairn
23 Beinn Sgritheall
24 Attadale Gardens
25 Craft Shop & Restaurant
26 Strathcarron Centre
27 Slumbay Harbour
28 Strome Castle
29 Lochcarron Weavers
30 Museum
Strathcarron
A896
Lochcarron
Attadale
Ardaneaskan
Loch Carron
Loch Reraig
A890
Plockton
Stromeferry
Duirinish
Sallachy
Erbusaig
Balmacara
Glen Elchaig
Kyle
Square
Ardelve
Camas
Luinie
Eilean Ban
A87
Dornie
Loch Alsh
Kintail
Totaig
Loch Duich
Morvich
Ratagan
Kyle Rhea
Glen Lichd
Glenelg
Glen mor
Shiel Bridge
Sound of Sleat
Balvraid
Sandaig Islands
Arnisdale
Loch Hourn
Corran

10. LOCHALSH

The region known as Lochalsh covers a much wider area than that simply bounded by Loch Alsh itself. It is a diverse and beautiful area, to which people return again and again simply because there is so much to see and do. It is rich in history. In 1263 King Haakon's fleet landed here from Norway but long before this ancient settlers had moved throughout the area, leaving as evidence large numbers of ancient burial places and fortifications which can still be seen.

The Skye Bridge

The Skye Bridge

Completed in 1995, The Skye Bridge is an elegant feat of engineering which hops from the Plock of Kyle onto Eilean Ban and then arcs across the seaward end of Loch Alsh. The complete bridge span is 570m (623 yards), not including the first "hop" onto Eilean Ban. It has been the subject of much controversy as, until the end of 2004, a toll was payable by visitors and residents alike. It was built by private enterprise but then bought back by the Scottish Executive in response to public resentment about the tolls.

The Kyle of Lochalsh

Known affectionately simply as "Kyle," this is a bustling place. Before the bridge was built this was the main departure point for ferries to Skye. It is from Kyle that the best views of the bridge are to be seen. Kyle is a busy working port. There are cafes, shops, a medical centre, tourist information, a swimming pool, fire station, supermarket, vet, dentist and a variety of accommodation. There are several tourist attractions which make it

The Kyle of Localsh

possible to happily spend a day here - rather than rushing off over the bridge to Skye which is what many people do when they have travelled this far! **Kyle Public Toilets** have the quirky distinction of being a tourist attraction in their own

Kyle public toilets !

World famous conveniences

right. Go and see for yourself! The **railway station**, as well as being the end of the line for Inverness/ Kyle trains, is the home of a small but interesting **railway museum**, restaurant and craft gallery. For anyone with time to spare the railway line north from Kyle, which is cut through sheer rock in places, must be one of the best in the country for stunning views. Nearby is the **lifeboat station** with a gift shop.

The Lifeboat Station & railway pier, Kyle

A boat trip on **Seaprobe Atlantis** offers a wonderful experience: a glazed viewing gallery allows people to explore underwater whilst remaining dry! For those arriving on their own boat, the pontoon in front of the **Kyle of Lochalsh Hotel** is the place to tie up. Excellent shower facilities are available at the nearby toilets.

The Kyle of Lochalsh Hotel

The Murchison Memorial

It is curious to find a memorial to a rent collector – but such is that to Donald Murchison. When his Jacobite landlord employer was exiled, Murchison continued to collect rent on his behalf. This was a dangerous job in view of the divided loyalties amongst the highlanders. The memorial is signposted from a lay-by on the A87 about a mile and a half east of Kyle.

The Lochalsh Woodland Garden, owned by the National Trust, is three miles east of Kyle and is a wonderfully peaceful place which occupies a beautiful loch side position and stretches down through woodland to the shore.

Balmacara Square

This is a pretty hamlet with a small development of shops situated in restored steadings which overlook an old mill pond. There is a small visitor centre and, for anyone interested in maps, **Caledonian Maps** who reproduce historical maps of Scotland. An alternative to returning to the A87 is to take the scenic road out of the Square towards **Erbusaig.**

Loch Long

From the A87 at **Ardelve** a minor road branches off to follow the western shore of Loch Long. Once a drove road, over which cattle used to be herded to the east coast, this is a place where time appears to have stood still. After three and a half miles the road arrives at the tiny hamlet of **Sallachy** overlooking the salt marshes near the head of the loch. The road continues a further three miles, crossing the river into the mouth of **Glen Elchaig**. A small car park at **Camas-Luinie** is the

Glen Elchaig

end of the road. For serious walkers this is the starting point of several different

Standing stones in Glen Elchaig

paths into the hills. For the less energetic it is a wonderful place to simply absorb the scenery, especially **Sguman Coinntich** towering across the glen, and to take the gentle walk along Glen Elchaig. (Stout shoes are a good idea as it can be quite boggy underfoot.) The rocks along the way are rich in beautiful mosses, rose coloured lichens and unusual ferns. A mysterious arrangement of small standing stones along the way is intriguing.

Dornie

Dornie is situated where **Loch Alsh** is joined by **Loch Duich and Loch Long**. It is a small village with a shop and post office and a variety of accommodation. From Dornie village a high level road leads to **Carr Brae Viewpoint**, overlooking Eilean Donan Castle. This

From Carr Brae Viewpoint

truly is the best angle of all from which to view what is reputedly the most photographed and filmed castle in the World.

Continuing along the road to rejoin the A87 near **Inverinate** affords what are arguably some of the best views in the area.

Eilean Donan Castle

Since the Sixth Century there has been a fortification on this site. However, the present castle was partly destroyed in the Eighteenth Century and lay in a state of ruin for nearly two centuries. The island and castle were bought by a private owner in 1911 and over the next twenty years it was restored, opening once more in 1932. The guided tours are lively and entertaining and the reconstruction of the castle kitchen (down to the potato

Eilean Donan Castle

peelings and the rats!) is superb. There is a large visitor centre with free parking, a cafe and an excellent gift shop.

Kintail

Kintail is designated as one of Scotland's great wilderness areas but even for those who do not wish to venture too far from the A87 it is an area of much interest and it is a shame to simply rush through on the main road.

From each end of the causeway across the head of Loch Duich a minor road leads off to the tiny settlement of Morvich. A short way along the northern road are the ruins of **Clachan Duich**, an ancient chapel which was in use until the mid Nineteenth Century. Traditionally members of the MacRae Clan were buried here and there are some interesting old tombstones. At Morvich there is a **National Trust Outdoor Centre** with information boards about the area. There is an exciting programme of Ranger-led walks in the summer months. The **River Croe** emerges here after winding its way down **Glen Lichd** below the famous **Five Sisters of Kintail,** Sgurr Fhuaran being the highest. (Three of the Five Sisters are higher than 3000' and therefore "Munroes.") Legend has it that the sisters waited in vain for five Irish princes to come and marry them but were then turned to stone. A track leads along the glen for a fairly easy walk with spectacular views and often sightings of deer grazing. This part of Kintail is a favourite haunt of Golden Eagles. Ptarmigan also breed amongst the mountains here but they are shy birds, preferring to stay on high ground.

The more determined can continue on into **Glen Affric** several miles further on, or to the 350' high **Falls of Glomach** – a strenuous walk (but worth the effort) to one of Scotland's highest waterfalls.

Beyond the causeway which carries the A87 across the top of Loch Duich is the **Kintail Lodge Hotel** with accommodation, bar, a bunk house and serving a full menu (including excellent fish and chips!)

Kintail Lodge Hotel

Nearby are The **Jacobite Restaurant** and a wonderfully quirky shop selling gifts and bric-a-brac. **Lochend Llama Treks** provide an interesting way to see the area.

Shiel Bridge
Shiel Bridge, at the bottom of Glen Shiel, has a filling station, camp site, a small shop and is where the road leads off along the southern shore of Loch Duich or to Glenelg.

Glenshiel
There are no less than twenty one Munroes in Glenshiel, the highest being A'Chralaig at 1120m. (3609') Glen Shiel is known for **The Battle of Glenshiel,** a notable Jacobite defeat in 1719 . The battle site is signposted from the A87 about half way down the glen, which follows the line of thc Old Military Road. There are several picnic sites signposted from the road.

The Cluanie Hotel is a homely landmark on a long stretch of uninhabited road. The bar offers a choice of over a hundred single malt whiskies and the hotel often hosts whisky tasting weekends.

Ratagan and Totaig
The tiny road which winds along the southern shore of Loch Duich passes through Ratagan and Letterfearn to end at Totaig, directly across the loch from Eilean Donan. At one time a ferry crossed the loch from here to Dornie and a small white ferry house remains. Beyond the road, after about half a mile along a well marked path, are the remains of a broch called **Caisteal Grugaig** which legend says was the home of a witch called Grugaig. An unusual feature of the broch is a triangular stone over the doorway. The path continues with the chance to see remote and pretty **Ardintoul Bay**. For the energetic, it is then possible to follow the path along the shoreline all the way to Glenelg.

The Glenelg Ferry

Glenelg

Glenelg
Glenelg is truly one of the planet's special places. It is beautiful, wonderfully remote and timeless. There are three ways to arrive here, each equally memorable: Firstly, one can walk (as above.) Secondly, one can drive from Glen Shiel, climbing a thousand feet above Loch Duich as the road twists and turns before dropping down to **General Wade's Military Road**. The third way is aboard the community owned, historical **Glenelg Ferry** across the fast running waters of narrow **Kyle Rhea** from Skye.

The village of Glenelg has a shop, post office, hotel and an informal campsite near the shore. Nearby are the ruins of a huge block of **military barracks** which were built in 1723 to house government troops sent to try and to quell the rebellious highlanders. Glenelg has a particularly imposing **War Memorial** right on the shore. Further along, signposted off to the left in Glen Beag, are the remains of one of the most intact **Iron Age brochs** in Britain, along with two further brochs. The double walls and parts of a flight of stairs survive. A little further up this road, near **Balvraid**, is a chambered cairn.

Iron Age broch

Along the coast from Glenelg are the **Sandaig Islands** where author **Gavin Maxwell** wrote "Ring of Bright Water." The road which follows the line of the coast continues along the shores of **Loch Hourne** and eventually to the tiny hamlets of **Arnisdale** and **Corran**. Above Arnisdale towers another of the area's Munroes, **Beinn Sgritheall**. At the end of the road is Corran, where a row of old crofting cottages survives on the shore, deer roam the village main street and

The Sandaig Islands

Corran

there is a very welcome cup of tea on offer in a rather unusual establishment.

"Milk, no sugar - please."

Duirinish

The minor road which heads north out of Kyle winds its way through some small hamlets, including Duirinish which has all the appearance of being trapped in a time warp. Two rows of white crofting cottages are separated by a stream, on the banks of which highland cattle can usually be seen grazing.

Plockton

Plockton is one of the area's prettiest villages with palm trees and tiny immaculate gardens across the road from the main street cottages. Overlooked by the imposing baronial **Duncraig Castle**, Plockton achieved fame as the setting for the TV series Hamish MacBeth. The sheltered bay provides a popular spot for

Plockton

visiting yachts. There is a general store, post office, several souvenir shops and a choice of excellent restaurants and a great takeaway. Bikes can be hired from the gift shop. Art exhibitions are held frequently in the village hall. Boat trips run from here to visit the resident seal colony.

Stromeferry (no ferry)

Yes, that appears to be its name – look out for the signpost! At one time a busy ferry service ran from Strome across **Loch Carron** but when the new road was built in 1971 the ferry became obsolete.

Attadale

Between Stromeferry and Strathcarron are the lovingly restored **Attadale Gardens**. Part of the 30,000 acre Attadale Estate, these are open to the public during the summer months. A selection of walks are detailed near the main entrance.

Strathcarron

Strathcarron is a small village situated at the head of Loch Carron. There is a hotel and restaurant here and the railway station houses the **Strathcarron Centre** where there is an exhibition, a post office, internet access and several small craft galleries.

Lochcarron

Lochcarron stretches along the northern shores of Loch Carron. It is in an idyllic location and it has a hotel, several

Strome Castle

restaurants and cafes, a filling station, a golf course and a sailing club at **Slumbay Harbour.** Lochcarron has its own annual Highland Games, usually held during mid July. A minor road continues along the shoreline past the ruins of Fifteenth Century **Strome Castle** perched on a headland beside the tiny, aptly named, **Castle Bay**. Beyond Castle Bay can be found **Lochcarron Weavers**, producing beautiful tartans.

At the end of the road is **Ardaneaskan** where there is a small parking area. Housed in an old croft house is a **museum** with various exhibits illustrating everyday Highland life of times gone by. Beyond the end of the road, a track continues to the head of one of Scotland's smallest sea lochs, **Loch Reraig**, which is an inlet of Loch Carron.

Public toilets can be found in the car park at the village hall, at Eilean Donan Castle, The Strathcarron Centre and Plockton. The World famous toilets at Kyle of Lochalsh really are worth a visit - even if you do not need to!

USEFUL INFORMATION

Telephone numbers
Police (emergency) 999 (or 112)
Broadford: 01471 822222
Dunvegan: 01470 521333
Kyle of Lochalsh: 01599 534222
Lochcarron: 01520 722222
Portree: 01478 612888
Uig: 01470 542222
Fire (emergency) 999 (or 112)
Ambulance (emergency) 999 (or 112)
Coastguard (emergency) 999 (or 112)
Mountain Rescue (emergency) 999 (or 112)
Hospitals Broadford: 01471 822491
Portree: 01478 613200
NHS 24 08454 242424
Dentists
Dunvegan: 01470 521774
Kyle of Lochalsh: 01599 534552, 01599 534726
Portree: 01478 612582, 01478 61277
Pharmacy Broadford: 01471 822235
Kyle of Lochalsh: 01599 534206
Portree: 01478 612100
Vets Broadford: 01471 822922
Skeabost: 01470 532385
Snizort: 01470 5332278
Tourist Information
Armadale: 01471 844249
Broadford: 01471 822361
Dunvegan: 01470 521581
Kyle of Lochalsh: 01845 225512
Portree: 01478 612137
Uig: 01470 542404
Bus Companies City Link: 08705 505050
Rapson's: 01463 710555
Trains
Kyle of Lochalsh, Plockton, Stomeferry and Strathcarron through 0845 7484950
Ferries Caledonian MacBrayne Ltd.
Armadale: 01471 844248
Mallaig: 01687 462403
Uig: 01470 542219
Glenelg Ferry, Kylerhea: 01599 511302

Breakdown recovery
Kyle (Morar Motors)01599 534329/534034
Portree Coachworks: 01478 612688
Taxis
Borve: A Taxi 01478 612323
Broadford: Waterloo Taxis 01471 822860
Dunvegan Taxis 01470 521560
Edinbane Taxis 01470 582327
Kyle Taxi Company 01599 534323
Mallaig: Franco's Taxis 01687 462800
Plockton Taxis 01599 544389
Portree: A1 Cabs 01478 611112
Dickie's Cabs 01478 613888
Don's Taxis 01478 613100
Gus's Taxis 01478 613000
Kenny's Taxis 01478 611844
South Skye: D. Nicholson 01471 844338

Ordnance Survey Maps
Road Map 2 Western Scotland & The Western Isles. Scale: 1: 250,000
Landranger Series. Scale 1:50,000
23 North Skye - Dunvegan & Portree
24 Raasay, Applecross, Loch Torridon & Plockton
25 Glen Carron & Glen Affric
32 South Skye & Cuillin Hills
33 Loch Alsh, Glen Shiel & Loch Hourn
Explorer Series. Scale 1:25,000
407 Skye - Dunvegan
408 Trotternish & The Storr
409 Raasay, Rona & Scaplay
410 Skye - Portree & Bracadale
411 Skye - Cuillin Hills
412 Skye - Sleat
413 Knoydart, Loch Hourn & Loch Duich
414 Glen Shiel & Kintail Forest
428 Kyle of Lochalsh, Plockton & Applecross
429 Glen Carron & West Morar

Bibliography:Skye & Its Legends: Otta Swire, The Place Names of Skye: J.MacDonald, Skye: Derek Cooper, Highways & Byways in the West Highlands: Seton Gordon